MELTDOWN

THE OFFICIAL

Fiery Foods Show Cookbook
and Chilehead Resource Guide

Dave DeWitt and Mary Jane Wilan
with Jeanette DeAnda

The Crossing Press
Freedom, CA

Books by Dave DeWitt and Mary Jane Wilan

The Food Lover's Handbook to the Southwest
Callaloo, Calypso, and Carnival: The Cuisines of Trinidad and Tobago
Hot & Spicy & Meatless (with Melissa T. Stock)
Hot & Spicy Chili (with Melissa T. Stock)
Hot & Spicy Latin Dishes (with Melissa T. Stock)

Acknowledgments

Hundreds of people have helped us over the years with the Fiery Foods Show and this book, and we gratefully thank all of you. However, a list of everyone would be too lengthy here. You know who you are, and we appreciate your dedication to the fiery foods industry.

Library of Congress Cataloging-in-Publication Data

DeWitt, Dave.
　　Meltdown: the official Fiery Foods Show cookbook and chilehead resource guide /
Dave DeWitt and Mary Jane Wilan with Jeanette DeAnda.
　　　　p.　cm.
　　Includes bibliographical references and index.
　　ISBN 0-89594-739-0 (pbk.)
　　1. Cookery (Hot pepper sauces) 2. Cookery, Caribbean. I. Wilan, Mary Jane.
II. DeAnda, Jeanette. III. Title.
TX819.H66D48　1995
641.6'384--dc20

94-48018
CIP

Contents

Introduction

We've had a lot of fun during the decade or so that we've been involved with hot and spicy foods, and it's time we shared some of it with you. This book focuses on a unique phenomenon in the field of packaged heat, a trade show that is also open to the general public. The reason for inviting both the trade and public to the same show is simple: we'd be lynched if we tried to keep the public out! Thousands and thousands of people look forward to this show every year, so they can stock up on their favorite products and sample all the new products that have come out. And, after all, the general public is perhaps the most important segment of the fiery foods industry—the consumers.

More than five hundred recipes from manufacturers and chefs were submitted for this book, but obviously we could not use all of them. So, we selected what we considered to be the best two hundred or so. We thank everyone for submitting and apologize if, during the lengthy editing process, some recipes were omitted. Also, because so many people were involved in the writing of the recipes, they needed to be standardized, which we have done.

We have attempted to compile the most useful book possible, and to that end we have included the resources necessary to dedicated chileheads. Among these are general mail-order catalogs for hot stuff, a listing of manufacturers and retailers who specialize in hot and spicy products, and even a list of our favorite hot and spicy books.

So, grab your favorite fiery foods products, and head to the kitchen. We'll show you how to cook with them! Anyone interested in further information on the National Fiery Foods Show should contact us at Sunbelt Shows, Inc., P.O. Box 4980, Albuquerque, New Mexico 87196-4980, (505) 873-9103, fax (505) 877-8579.

The Hottest Show on Earth

Welcome to a world where the food bites you back! It's variously called the chile pepper industry and the hot and spicy business, but we call it fiery foods. It is, quite simply, a paradigm shift in the way North Americans are eating and could be the most significant change in eating habits in the history of the United States and Canada.

The Fiery Foods Explosion

The term fiery food was coined in 1975 by John Philips Cranwell, the author of *The Hellfire Cookbook*, which, we believe, was the first cookbook devoted exclusively to hot and spicy foods. "Fiery food, like alcohol, is habit-forming," Cranwell wrote. "If you accustom yourself to neat whiskey, you will not again be completely satisfied with watered strong waters; once you have acquired a taste for fiery food, you will never again be satisfied with bland fare."

Of course, manufactured fiery foods have been around a lot longer than twenty years (Tabasco sauce was first bottled in 1868), so it might seem strange that only during the past two decades has their popularity reached such a height that we now have a magazine about the subject, plus a trade show, dozens of festivals, mail-order companies, and retail shops devoted to hot and spicy. How—and why—did this explosion happen?

Before 1975, fiery foods were popular primarily in two parts of this country: the Southwest and southern Louisiana. People in these regions knew what the rest of the world has known for centuries: that chile peppers are tasty and good for you, and that they can spice up bland staples such as rice, corn, and beans. But during the past two decades, hot and spicy dishes have broken free from their regional roots and swept the country. First Cajun food, then Southwestern and Mexican, and finally Asian food has become popular from Oregon to Key West, from Hawaii to Maine. There are many reasons for this pungent phenomenon:

Changing immigration patterns. During the eighteenth and nineteenth centuries, the vast majority of new American and Canadian citizens arrived from Europe, which, with the exception of Hungary, is not noted for spicy food. But during the twentieth century, the majority of immigrants came from regions that are noted for spicy food— especially Mexico and Latin America, the Caribbean, and Southeast Asia. These immigrants brought their culture and food habits with them. They opened markets and restaurants, and soon North Americans were giving them a try.

More adventurous American eating. People are still eating meat and potatoes, but now they're slathering them with salsa! We often hear about the horrors of fast food and how it's destroying our taste buds, but there's another side to the story. Cooking has become more of a hobby than a necessity, specialty and ethnic restaurants have sprung up everywhere, and people have become more daring in their eating habits. Although for centuries some of us have eaten raw oysters, the thought of eating sashimi or sushi was shocking until fairly recently. In fact, the willingness of North Americans to eat raw fish parallels the rise of spicy foods. And as anyone who has even dipped their raw fish in wasabi will tell you, hot and spicy goes well with sashimi!

Greater foreign travel. The willingness of North Americans to experiment with new foods can be seen at the Double-V Jerk Centre in Ocho Rios, Jamaica, where vanloads of tourists wolf down the Scotch bonnet-infused jerk pork alongside the locals, while reggae music pounds through the speakers. After experiencing such foods on vacation, people wish to re-create the tastes at home. This accounts for much of the popularity, for example, of jerk sauces, which were almost unknown in this country a few years ago.

Greater availability of chiles. One of the biggest problems in the early days of the hot and spicy movement was finding the principal ingredients. This is not so any longer, with fresh habaneros appearing in supermarkets and an astounding variety of dried chiles available by mail order. Except for the South American ajís and rocotos, most of the important chiles from around the world can now be easily had. In Austin's fabulous Central Market, we counted nine varieties of dried chiles and eight of fresh chiles! Incidentally, home gardeners have also helped the hot and spicy trend, and seeds of all five domesticated species (with dozens and dozens of varieties) are now available.

The cookbook explosion. Between 1975 and mid-1994, thirty-three collections of hot and spicy recipes were published. This total does not include books on specific fiery cuisines such as Thai, Caribbean, and Mexican. The popularity of fiery foods is reflected in the books devoted to them—including this one.

One of the most commonly asked questions about fiery foods is this: What is the dollar volume of the industry? There are three problems in estimating the size of the fiery foods industry. One is determining the bounds of a broad industry that begins with agriculture and ends with food processing and even the manufacture of nonfood items, such as chile pepper T-shirts. The second problem is that no one is tracking all the figures, so educated guesses still predominate in any calculations. The third problem is that many fiery foods companies are privately held—Tabasco's

McIlhenny Company comes to mind—and do not release sales figures.

In 1989 we endeavored to estimate the size of the fiery foods industry—a task that proved to be rather frustrating because of the above constraints. First we divided the industry into its component parts: fresh produce, manufactured products, and miscellaneous and nonfood items. Then we attempted to find statistics to match each category within these parts, such as canned chiles, pickled peppers, frozen foods, and so on. Some statistics, such as supermarket salsa sales, were easy to find, but others, such as gourmet shop salsa sales, were impossible to obtain; we had to estimate. Finally, after all the collected figures and estimates were added up, the total came to $1.71 billion in sales.

Then we realized that we had not included every segment of the industry, such as food service sales and foreign sales. Given this oversight and the spectacular growth of the industry (supermarket salsa sales nearly doubled in three years, from about $400 million in 1989 to about $700 million in 1992), we can roughly estimate the value of the fiery foods industry in 1995 at about $2.5 billion.

The companies represented by the industry range in size from small mom-and-pop operations each manufacturing a single spicy salsa to giants such as Pet Old El Paso. And where do they all get together to do business and have a hot time? Why, at the Fiery Foods Show, of course.

It's Show Time

A combination of happenstance, frustration, and sheer luck led to the first National Fiery Foods Show, held September 9-11, 1988. In February of that year, Dave DeWitt attended the New Mexico Chile Conference in Las Cruces and noticed that some of the sponsors of the conference had small tabletop displays of their products and services. Bingo! Inspired, he thought: Why not a trade show for the chile-pepper industry?

That moment was the happenstance because Dave had been a show producer since 1972, when he produced the Bargain Days Flea Market, in Richmond, Virginia. In the years that followed, Dave had produced antique shows and many custom car shows, but he had never even been to a food show, much less produced one. The frustration, in fact, occurred because of a custom car show. In 1987, Dave had coproduced (with Frank Crosby), the Miller Motorsports Expo, a charity event to benefit Congressman Manuel Lujan's Excellence in Education scholarship program. At that show, he met and became friends with Dave and Barbara Schrader, who were showing their sports cars. The Daves became determined to produce a similar event in El Paso, but problems in getting a hall and sponsors forced them to cancel the event.

DeWitt suggested the idea of a show for the chile pepper industry to Schrader, who lived in El Paso. Schrader, a former linebacker for the Chicago Bears and a mortgage banker, loved the idea. For both Daves, the frustration about the canceled show was replaced by anticipation. They planned the show for the fall in El Paso, when the chile harvest would be under way in southern New Mexico.

The sheer luck part of the show was that DeWitt had also teamed up with another partner in his life, Mary Jane Wilan, who turned out to be an ideal show producer. At that time, Mary Jane was teaching English to seniors at Manzano High School—but she had the summer off and could and would sell booth space in the show.

The three partners jumped into action. We rented the ballroom at the El Paso Hilton and printed a brochure about the show. A close friend, Wayne Scheiner, came up with the slogan: "The Hottest Show on Earth." The exhibitor's rate was $250 for an 8-by 10-foot booth.

Despite advance publicity through the *Albuquerque Journal* and the *El Paso Times*, the first Fiery Foods Show was not an easy sell. The show had no track record, and it was difficult to convince potential exhibitors that they were part of a larger products industry. It would take years before such divergent groups as the New Mexico chile producers, the Louisiana hot sauce manufacturers, and importers of Caribbean and Asian products would realize that they were all part of the fiery foods industry, as it would be called after the first show.

Another problem with selling the show was that *Chile Pepper* magazine was in its infancy and was not yet the powerful promotional vehicle it would become. That summer Robert Spiegel had just published his third issue, and our advertising reached only a fraction of the industry. But we had Mary Jane on the phone, and she sweet-talked company owners into exhibiting. Although we didn't fill the hall, we ended up with 37 exhibitors in 42 booths (since a trade-show exhibitor may rent two or three booths or share a booth with another exhibitor, the number of exhibitors seldom matches the number of spaces).

We spread out the decorated booths as best we could and waited for the crowds to pour in. "Trickle in" would be a better description; as one exhibitor later commented, "You could have rolled a bowling ball down the aisles and not hit anyone." This was an exaggeration, but only about five hundred people visited the show over the weekend.

But none of the exhibitors seemed to mind. They appeared to be happy just being a part of this unique event. After all, we had some fiery-foods celebrities in attendance: Harold Timber, who had recently won the $10,000 top prize at the International Chili Society (ICS) World's Championship Chili Cookoff, and Jane Butel, the author of spicy cookbooks and a spice manufacturer. And Dr. Paul Bosland, who had recently taken over the chile-breeding program at New Mexico State University, entertained the attendees and exhibitors with his chile displays.

Some of the exhibitors present who have been in nearly every show since were Old Southwest Trading Company, Bueno Foods, and Sauces and Salsas, Ltd. Attending but not exhibiting were Jeff Campbell of Stonewall Chili Pepper Company and Robert Mahan of Mahan's Southwest Gourmet Sauces. Our show sponsors that year were the same as in the 1994 show: Coca-Cola and Budweiser. Some of the more interesting products displayed were jalapeño wine from Domingo and the Gringo (the gringo being Keith "Doc" Shepherd) and chile-cured caviar steeped in Absolut Peppar Vodka from the Carolyn Collins Caviar Company.

One particularly funny incident occurred. Jeff Campbell, the habanero grower and food manufacturer, had brought a bag of fresh habaneros with him. They were quite a hit; the other exhibitors had heard of the peppers but had never seen them—much less tasted them. A few brave souls tasted small sections of the habaneros that Jeff cut up, but Patrick Dwyer, an exhibitor from Washington, D.C., whose company was called Not For Wimps, bragged that he could eat a whole pod! Grinning, Jeff handed him one. Patrick popped the orange pod into his mouth and chewed it up.

His eyes bulged and tears formed. His face got red. Perspiration beaded up on his forehead and began running down his nose. But he didn't choke, and he didn't spit it out. The admiring crowd applauded as Patrick walked away—a little unsteadily. Interestingly enough, Patrick never returned to another Fiery Foods Show!

After the show ended, the two Daves did an accounting to see how much money they had lost. Surprisingly, the crowds were slightly larger than we had thought, and we made a profit—about a hundred dollars, but still a profit.

The after-show publicity was strong. "They came to stoke the fire," wrote Susan Stiger, the food editor of the *Albuquerque Journal*, in a strongly positive article entitled "Power to the Pod." The article featured a full-color photo of DeWitt in a sombrero giving a "power to the people" salute with a fresh New Mexican chile pod. This first big article gained us a footing for the next show. But we also recognized that the show had to be restructured.

The two main problems with the show were the dates and the location. In the late summer and fall growers and processors are too busy with the harvest to attend shows, and manufacturers and retailers are preoccupied with back-to-school sales and the impending Christmas season. We decided to move the show to February, making it one of the first food shows of the season, about a month before the winter Fancy Food Show on the West Coast. But since we didn't have enough time between September and February to produce the second show, we were forced to schedule the second show eighteen months after the first one.

The change in locations was for personal reasons. Dave Schrader was too busy with his business to coproduce any longer, so Dave and Mary Jane decided to move the show to their home town of Albuquerque. We had produced most of our other shows in that city and knew the market well. Although many other hot and spicy cities, including Santa Fe, Las Cruces, Austin, San Antonio, Tucson, Phoenix, and New Orleans could have hosted the Fiery Foods Show, Albuquerque was the most logical choice for us.

We selected the ballroom at the Holiday Inn Journal Center (called the Pyramid because of its Aztec design), because it was the largest private facility available in the city. We didn't think that we were ready for the Convention Center yet.

Our third change for the second show was in the days of the week it would run: Saturday, Sunday, and Monday instead of Friday, Saturday, and Sunday. We did this on the advice of one our exhibitors in the first show, who told us that retail buyers didn't want to waste their weekend attending a show, but would attend on a weekday. So, the schedule called for us to admit the general public only on Sunday and reserve Monday for trade attendees.

The second show was held February 10-12, 1990. Because we had eighteen months to promote the show and also because of the growing interest in *Chile Pepper* magazine, in which we placed most of our trade advertising, the number of exhibitors more than doubled, to 76 exhibitors in 69 booths. We also radically increased our radio and newspaper advertising. Attendance was light on Saturday but very heavy on Sunday. Monday was very slow, proving that the new schedule wasn't working. Live and learn.

Despite some problems, the second show was a much bigger success than the first one. Total attendance reached nearly two thousand. We began our cooking demonstrations, and some of the first guest chefs (notably Todd Sanson, W.C. Longacre, and Eddie Adams) have been with us since then. Unusual products included Adelina Willem's red and green chile pastas and a red chile honey from Taos. Another notable development was that the Caribbean contingent began to participate, with products from Grenada, Trinidad, Belize, and Jamaica. Our first exhibitor with hot and spicy Asian products, Lee Kum Kee International, also participated.

Despite the poor attendance on Monday, we were buoyed by a front-page article that same day in the *Albuquerque Journal*. Again by Susan Stiger, this one began: "There was a fire Sunday. But the only damage was to tongues."

The next step for the show was to move to larger facilities at the Albuquerque Convention Center. We still didn't think we were ready for the 30,000-square-foot exhibit halls, so we opted for the combined meeting rooms in the new addition to the center. That space was about 20 percent larger than the ballroom at the Pyramid.

We set the dates as February 15-17, 1991—back to Friday, Saturday, and Sunday. Mary Jane coined a nickname for the show, "The Meltdown!," and we have used it ever since 1991. Our third show featured 95 exhibitors in 79 booths, and many distributors showed up representing many manufacturers.

We enjoyed our first coverage by Associated Press, with articles about the show appearing in more than one hundred U.S. newspapers and even in the European edition of *The Stars and Stripes*. David Plotnikoff wrote in the *Los Angeles Times*: "And for the true believers, Meltdown is the culinary equivalent to a trip to Mecca—the ultimate step in the never-ending quest for fire."

There was plenty of fire—and plenty of chile-heads to enjoy it, as attendance increased by about a thousand people despite some resistance to long-distance travel because of the Gulf War. Ormly Gumfudgin, the ICS historian who tended a huge pot of chili at the show, said to Plotnikoff about the public's ability to eat spicy food, "You know, some of these people here are just a bit extreme."

Our third show brought new exhibitors, including José Marmolejo, the Mexican chile importer; four California wineries; Shepherd's Garden Seeds; and our first book publisher, Ten Speed Press which was selling Mark Miller's posters and books—and had him there to sign them. Unusual products included a jalapeño honey mustard from Desert Farms; hot and spicy pistachios from Heart of the Desert; hot and spicy candies from Pat's Pending Company and Windmill Candy, chile and lime potato chips from Saguaro Potato Chips of Tucson; and pineapple salsa from Santa Fe Exotix.

Perhaps the highlight of the show was two guys who drove all the way from Philadelphia with the slogan "Heat-Seeking Missile" painted on the side of their car.

We moved our fourth show, February 7-9, 1992, to the Northwest Hall of the Albuquerque Convention Center but we were able to fill only about two-thirds of the hall. It was an unusual show in that we sold more booths than before but to fewer exhibitors—76 exhibitors in 83 booths. Thanks to advance publicity through *USA Today*'s long article, "Chile Peppers Catch Fire with U.S. Palates," attendance by tradespeople increased greatly, and total attendance nearly doubled, to about five thousand.

New chefs doing cooking demonstrations included Rosa Rajkovic, a James Beard Award nominee for Best Southwest Chef; FoFo Voltaire, cooking Caribbean specialties; Susan Richmond from the Sheraton Grande Torrey Pines Resort in

La Jolla; and the food editor of *Chile Pepper*, Nancy Gerlach. Unusual products at the show were Slightly Spicy Toffee Almonds from Fresh Pleasures; Mrs. Dog's Disappearing Mustard; and Pikled Garlik. Silliker Laboratories offered manufacturers high-performance liquid chromatography (HPLC) testing of products, Steven Kilbourn's pepper motif pottery was a hit, and the extremely hot habanero paste from Virgin Islands Herb and Pepper Company stunned everyone.

The publicity continued to increase. Another Associated Press article ran in hundreds of newspapers across the country. Cable News Network ran a lengthy report on the show, and *The New Yorker* sent Jane and Michael Stern, well-known food writers, to cover the show. Their article was one of the best descriptions of the show ever published.

Caribbean Food Products won the Best Hot Sauce award in the Fiery Foods Challenge with their Trinidad Habanero Pepper Sauce, and that win netted a front-page article in the Trinidad and Tobago *Daily Express* with the headline "The Hottest Peppersauce in the World."

Attendance continued to increase by about a thousand people per show for the next two years. Our fifth show, held February 12-14, 1993, filled 85 percent of the Northwest Hall; we had 103 exhibitors in 105 booths. But we almost had a scandal besides. In a preview article about the show, the *Albuquerque Tribune* announced that an exhibitor would be cooking "live baby eels in chile sauce." We received several angry calls from animal rights activists, but they calmed down when we assured them that not only were eels out of season, they had never been found in the Rio Grande. We don't know where the reporter for the *Trib* came up with that one—although such a dish, for Spanish anguilas, was mentioned in 1988 in *Chile Pepper* magazine.

The unusual products at our fifth show included Sri Lankan curry pastes from Nature's Key; Crazy Ed's Cave Creek Chili Beer; Dat'l Do It Hot Sauces, made with datil peppers from St. Augustine, Florida; Dave's Insanity Sauce; Outerbridge Sherry Pepper Sauce from Bermuda; Satay Indonesian condiments; and Jalapeño-Garlic Goat Cheese from Sweetwood's Dairy.

New chefs were Farn Boggie, from the Piñon Grill in Scottsdale; Jim Heywood, from the Culinary Institute of America; Tita Libin, a Mexican cookbook author from Cuernavaca; and Lois Ellen Frank, cook and photographer, who photographed the famous Mark Miller chile posters.

And we finally made *The Wall Street Journal*. In an article entitled "Chile Heads in Their Element," Harlan Clifford wrote, "The smell was the clue. Rich and powerful, it billowed out the door of the convention hall here: the tang of hot peppers." The show was also covered at length by Bill Geist of "CBS Sunday Morning with Charles Kuralt." He was astounded by the number and variety of products on display and enjoyed hunting for burned-out attendees.

Our sixth show, held February 18-20, 1994, got off to the right start with advance coverage by Richard Lerner in the Sunday *New York Times*. "With over a hundred exhibitors using two dozen varieties of chiles, the festival is a testament not only to the appeal that has made salsa a challenge to ketchup's supremacy, but also to the seductive nature of food itself."

With exhibitors in 123 booths, we completely filled the Southwest Hall, which is the same size as the Northwest Hall, thirty thousand square feet. We had a waiting list of more than twenty companies. We also had the largest crowds ever—the aisles were constantly jammed. Our number of international exhibitors continued to grow, and we expanded our show program to include some articles from trade journals and statistics on fiery foods sales. Chefs demonstrating were Scott Landry, from Lake Charles, Louisiana; Lora Brody, from Boston; Jay McCarthy, from Cascabel in San Antonio; and Donna Nordin, from Cafe Terra Cotta in Tucson.

Among the exhibitors were more publishers of hot and spicy cookbooks, including Border Books, Canyonlands Publications, Crossing Press, Golden West Publishers, and Ten Speed Press. Unusual products were Habanero Garlic-Stuffed Olives from Gil's Gourmet Gallery; Green Chile Turkey sausage from the Grocery Emporium; Hogg Wild Chili Fixins from Hi-Co Western Products; Red Chile Bread Mix from Mannon's Foods; and Green Chile Pretzels from Santa Fe Cookie Company.

Perhaps the most unusual story we can tell about a product concerned Dave's Insanity Sauce. This sauce is made with capsicum oleoresin, a chemical extract from chiles that is very high in capsaicin. Because some unpleasant reactions in 1993 caused some complaints, we requested that Dave Hirschkopf not give tastings of the Insanity Sauce. He could, however, sell unopened bottles. Instead of taking offense at such rules, Hirschkopf responded in true entrepreneurial fashion: he dressed in a strait jacket and put up large signs saying "Banned from the Fiery Foods Show." Incidentally, he also told the Albuquerque Tribune, "A true chilehead goes for an endorphin rush— he goes for sensation, not flavor." We hope he was kidding.

We were grateful for coverage after the show by Associated Press (again), WFAA-TV in Fort Worth, the TV Food Network, the *Boston Globe*, and the *Columbus Dispatch*. Attendance topped seven thousand, and we made plans to move to the much larger Northeast Hall.

We would be remiss not to mention the non-food products, besides books, that have appeared in our shows over the years. Because of the enormous popularity of chile peppers, we have seen them emblazoned upon T-shirts, towels, napkins, cards, magnets, windsocks, aprons, plates, door knockers, jewelry, underpants, halter tops, and even pasties.

Our favorite names among fiery food products speak of power: Revenge, Swamp Bite, Heat Wave, Religious Experience, Whiplash, No Joke, Pure Hell, The Wrath, Atomic Bob's, Wildfire, El Diablo, Devil Drops, Hell in a Bottle, Desert Devil, Virgin Fire, Scorned Woman, Texas Tears, TNT, Gunpowder, Spitfire, Snakebite, Voodoo, and Satan's Revenge.

The Rise and Fall of the Fiery Foods Challenge

It seemed like a good idea at first—let the public vote for their favorite hot and spicy products and give award certificates to the winning companies. We did so during our first show, in 1988, when we only had 37 exhibitors, and the single category was Best Salsa. Because of the small number of exhibitors and the low attendance, it was easy to count the votes even before the show ended. The winner? OG's Tortilla Factory (now out of business).

During our second show, we retained the one category, Best Salsa, and counting the ballots was still relatively easy. OG's won for the second year in a row.

We increased the categories to three for our third show—Best Salsa, Best Hot Sauce, and Best Marinade/BBQ Sauce—and our troubles began. Mary Jane complained that there was not enough time to count the hundreds and hundreds of ballots before the show ended. And there was the problem of ballot stuffing. Despite the fact that the ballots were printed in the show program, some exhibitors collected them by the dozens and voted for their own products. It was easy to spot the stuffed ballots—wadded together, all filled out in the same handwriting with the same color of ink, voting for a single product. We did not count the stuffed ballots, and we made some plans to control stuffing for the next year. Oh, and OG's won Best Salsa for the third year in a row.

For our fourth show, we decided to pass out a ballot at the door to each attendee. We also planned to wait until after the show to count the ballots, and then to announce the winners to the media. At exhibitors' suggestion, we increased the award categories to five, adding Most Unusual Product and Best Overall Product. More problems cropped up. Before the show opened on Saturday morning, Dave caught one of the exhibitors stealing several packs of ballots, and, in an unpleasant confrontation, demanded their return. The exhibitor reluctantly agreed after protesting that he had the right to vote for his own product. "Four hundred times?" Dave asked him.

The fifth show was comparatively calm, but because of the problems we'd had with ballot stuffing in the past, we hired two extra employees to do nothing but pass out ballots. Since some exhibitors had complained that not enough awards were given in the competition, we allowed five instead of three winners in each category.

For the sixth annual show, held in 1994, Mary Jane, who by then was very weary of counting thousands of votes, wanted to cancel the Fiery Foods Challenge. But Dave gave in to pressure from exhibitors. We separated the barbecue sauce and marinade categories and added Best Mustard and Best Jam/Jelly. We now had eight categories and five places in each category, which meant that as many as forty companies could win awards. Things were getting out of hand. Some exhibitors griped that we were not doing enough to promote the winners, but we countered that the contest was secondary to the show and that any promotion should be done by the winners, not by the producers.

The 1994 Fiery Foods Challenge was a zoo. Aggressive exhibitors begged and hounded attendees to vote for them; they seemed to think that the voting was more important than selling their own products. Interestingly enough, although in 1994 general attendance was considerably higher than in 1993, the total number of ballots cast for products was down, and ballot stuffing was virtually nonexistent. We believe that the attendees were overwhelmed by the number of categories—and the number of different products in the show (between four hundred and five hundred) made it difficult for them to do an objective sampling. Many attendees did not take the voting seriously: on quite a few ballots, Budweiser or cold water was voted Best Overall Product.

After the show, the hot sauce hit the fan. One disgruntled exhibitor, who had won a first-place award in 1993 but only a second place in 1994, complained bitterly. We told him that he legitimately finished second, and that we could not change the results. He argued that there were too few categories and we ought to divide the Best

Salsa category into fresh salsa, bottled salsa, and salsa mixes. How many salsa categories can there be, we asked him, twenty? Fifty? Did we really want a category like "Best West Texas Bottled Salsa?"

About a week after the show, we received a fax from the exhibitor's attorney demanding a "recount and a canvass of the ballots." That was the last straw. Since the ballots were by then under tons of trash at the landfill, we couldn't comply even if we wanted to. We put the demand "under advisement in the circular file" and reevaluated the Fiery Foods Challenge.

It was now evident that we had created a monster. Our purpose in producing the Fiery Foods Show was to bring people together to sell products, find distributors, and exchange information, and not to conduct a popularity contest. We concluded that a few exhibitors had spoiled the competition for the others, and that we were tired of dealing with all the problems that accompanied the voting. So, after six years, we eliminated the Fiery Foods Challenge—it had gone from a friendly tasting competition to a battle fought through faxes from lawyers. It was time to kill the monster and concentrate on the future of the Fiery Foods show.

And what is that future? Continued growth, we hope. Because the 1994 show sold out of booth space more than a month before the event, we moved the show across the street to a larger hall, in the new part of the Albuquerque Convention Center, with room for 180 exhibitors. At this writing, more and more hot and spicy products debut every week, and fiery foods have gained popularity in all regions of North America. We recall the words of John Philips Cranwell, and fervently hope they are as true as they seem to be: "Once you have acquired a taste for fiery food, you will never again be satisfied with bland fare." And, whenever we get aggravated, as we did with the Fiery Foods Challenge, we also recall the words of longtime exhibitor Chuck Evans: "Remember El Paso!"

About the Products in the Recipes

Obviously, this cookbook is designed to be used mostly with manufactured hot and spicy products. Although some are starting to appear in supermarkets, the greatest selection is usually found in specialty gourmet shops and mail-order catalogs. To track down the various products used in this book, we suggest beginning with the gourmet shops in your area. Pay them a visit to find out which hot and spicy products they carry, and if they don't have your personal favorites, suggest that they try them. Some shops specialize in fiery foods. We've listed some of these in "Resources," but the list is by no means complete; fiery foods shops are springing up everywhere.

If you can't find what you're looking for in local shops, the next step is to order the mail-order catalogs listed in "Resources," as they generally have the widest selection of products. Finally, if the catalogs don't have what you want, try the manufacturer. Check the recipe introduction for the name of the manufacturer (which may differ from the name of the product), and then look up the manufacturer in "Resources." Many manufacturers sell their products by mail; if they don't, they know who does.

Although the recipes are designed to be used with the products indicated in italics, we have indicated the approximate substitutions that will provide a similar—but not exact—taste. In the case of brand-name dried chiles or powders, simply substitute another brand of the same variety. Following is the key for substitutions.

Substitution Key

A = Any dry salsa or spice mix

B = Any bottled tomato-based salsa

C = Any chile-infused vinegar

D = Any liquid hot pepper sauce

E = Any hot and spicy nuts

F = Any hot and spicy barbecue sauce

G = Any habanero hot sauce

H = Any hot and spicy mustard

I = Any curry sauce

J = Any fruit salsa

K = Any pepper jelly

L = Any chile paste

M = Any hot and spicy grilling sauce or marinade

N = Any Cajun spice mix

O = Any chile con carne dry mix

P = Any sherry pepper sauce

Q = Any jerk paste or dry jerk spice mix

R = Any hot and spicy pesto

S = Any chile-infused vegetable oil

T = Any chile pasta

U = Any hot and spicy chutney

The Heat Scales

The heat scale for each recipe is indicated by a graphic of a hot sauce bottle, according to the following ratings:

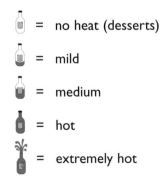

= no heat (desserts)

= mild

= medium

= hot

= extremely hot

Sizzling Starters

moky Chipotle Salsa Dip

The intriguing flavor of these dried smoked jalapeño chiles creates a memorable salsa with true south of the border flair. This fine product which contains the dried chipotles and a spice mix is created by Angel Sustaeta of Chile Bravo! Imports, in Phoenix, Arizona.

**1 package *Smoky Chipotle Salsa Spice Mix*
  (or substitute dried chipotles and A)**
2 cups water
1 lime
1 tablespoon red wine vinegar
4 cups Italian tomato halves

Remove the chipotle chiles from the package. In a saucepan, bring the water to a boil. Remove the pan from the heat, and place the chiles in the pan until they are rehydrated (approximately 15 to 20 minutes). Drain the chiles, let them cool, and remove their stems and seeds. Purée the chiles, lime, and vinegar in a blender or food processor.

Preheat the oven to 350 degrees. Put the tomatoes into a baking pan, and bake them until they are tender, approximately 20 minutes. Blend in the spice mix, remove the salsa to a serving bowl, and let the salsa sit for one hour at room temperature.

Serve the salsa with chips.

Serves 4 to 6

Sundance Artichoke Dip

Not only is this dip easy to make, it is also rich and delicious. The recipe was contributed by Sundance Foods of Bay View, Wisconsin.

1 cup mayonnaise
1 cup grated Parmesan cheese
**1 3/4 cups canned artichoke hearts,
  drained and chopped**
**1 tablespoon dry *Sundance Salsa Blend*,
  (or substitute A)**

Preheat the oven to 350 degrees. In a bowl, mix all the ingredients. Spoon the mixture into a 9-inch pie plate. Bake 20 to 25 minutes, or until the mixture is lightly browned. Serve it hot, with tortilla chips, crackers, or pita bread wedges.

Variation: Add 8 ounces of canned crab meat to the mixture before baking, or after baking, sprinkle the top with 2 tablespoons green onion slices and 2 tablespoons chopped tomato.

Yields 2 1/2 cups

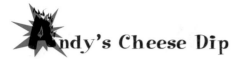ndy's Cheese Dip

This hearty dip is great served with either corn or flour tortilla chips, or used as a sauce with vegetables, pasta, or potatoes. Andy's zesty salsa really brings other foods to life. You may prefer to use proportionately less meat or cheese than called for here.

1 pound lean ground beef
1/2 pound sausage meat
   (preferably Jimmy Dean)
1 pound American or medium
   cheddar cheese
1/4 cup *Andy's Southern Salsa* (hot or mild)
   (or substitute B)

In a skillet, brown the ground beef and sausage. While the meat is browning, heat the cheese in a saucepan, stirring often, just until the cheese is completely melted. Drain the fat from the meat, and stir in first the cheese, then the salsa. Serve the dip hot.

Serves 4

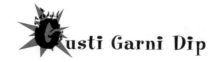usti Garni Dip

Stacy Tanner, the owner of Bowman's Landing Epicurean Company in Hinsdale, Illinois, has some great recipes; they are easy and elegant, and allow you to relax and enjoy your guests. This recipe can be doubled.

1 3/4 cups canned artichoke hearts,
   chopped fine
2 tablespoons *Gusti Garni Vinegar*
   (or substitute C)
1 tablespoon grated Parmesan cheese
1/8 teaspoon dried oregano
1/8 teaspoon dried basil
1/8 teaspoon garlic powder

Mix all the ingredients well, a day before serving, if possible.

Serve the mixture with crackers and veggie sticks.

Serves 4 to 6

eviled Corn Dip

This tasty dip can be served cold or hot. The combination of flavors is terrific, and chances are that once you try this dip, you'll make it again and again! Joe Dulle's Rio Diablo Company is located in Austin, Texas—home of the famous Austin Chronicle Hot Sauce Contest.

**1 1/2 cups corn kernels, cooked and
   drained
3/4 cup grated extra sharp cheddar cheese
2 tablespoons sour cream
3/4 cup *Rio Diablo Salsa* (or substitute B)**

Mix all the ingredients together. Start dipping immediately or heat the mixture gently in a saucepan before serving.

Serves 4

ot Crab Dip

You've got to try this great seafood appetizer. Serve it with pita wedges, fried wontons, or tortilla chips. For an interesting twist, Kathleen Redle of Century Sauce Kitchens suggests also accompanying the dip with fresh fruit or vegetables.

**1 pound cream cheese, softened
1/2 teaspoon Old Bay Seasoning
1/2 teaspoon sugar
Juice of 1/2 lemon
1/4 cup *Century Hot Pepper Sauce*
   (or substitute D)
2 cups fresh or frozen crabmeat
Cayenne powder, to taste**

In a bowl, combine the first five ingredients. Gently fold in the crabmeat, and stir until the ingredients are well combined. Spread the mixture in a shallow broiler-proof baking dish and dust with cayenne pepper. Broil for 10 minutes, or until the dip is brown on top and bubbling. Serve it immediately.

Serves 4 to 6

 **ip Jarocho**

We are always happy to receive recipes using chipotle chiles, which provide a wonderful smoky complement to most foods. This unusual dip is simple to prepare. We thank Angel Sustaeta, of Chile Bravo! Imports, for the recipe.

4 Avante jarred Chipotle Chiles
8 to 10 garlic cloves, minced
1/2 cup juice from chiles
2 tablespoons sugar
1 cup mayonnaise

Blend all of the ingredients. Serve as a dip for shrimp or chips, or as a sauce for pasta or vegetables.

Serves 4

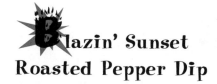 **lazin' Sunset Roasted Pepper Dip**

Tim Fex of Blazin' Oregon Food Products has created a real winner here. This dip is not only delicious; it is beautiful to look at. Roasting the peppers, under a broiler or over the flame of a gas stove, imparts a special flavor to the dip.

2 yellow bell peppers, roasted, peeled, seeded, and chopped
2 red bell peppers, roasted, peeled, seeded, and chopped
8 large garlic cloves, peeled and roasted in the oven for about 20 minutes and chopped
1/2 cup Blazin' Oregon Hot Hazelnuts (or substitute E)
1 tablespoon olive oil
1/2 teaspoon vinegar
1/4 teaspoon ground cumin
Cayenne powder to taste

Mince together the yellow bell peppers, hazelnuts, and half the garlic in a food processor. Scrape the sides and add 1 1/2 teaspoons oil, 1/4 teaspoon vinegar and 1/8 teaspoon cumin, and a dash of cayenne powder, and purée until the mixture is smooth but not thin. Place it in a bowl, and set the bowl aside. Repeat this process using the red bell peppers. The dip can be served in a shallow bowl with one half designed in yellow and the other side designed in red.

Serves 4 to 6

ool Saguaro Dip Mix

Cool green like the Saguaro cactus, this mild oregano-flavored spice mix makes a tasty spread that can also be used as a delicious stuffing for chicken or seafood. Chef Donna Nordin, owner of the famous Cafe Terra Cotta in Tucson, has created a great line of products. She also suggests serving the dip with crackers, bread, chips, or fruits and vegetables.

1 pound cream cheese, softened
1/2 cup milk or cream
2 tablespoons lemon juice
3 tablespoons olive oil
1 package *Terra Cotta Cool Saguaro Dip Mix*
  (or substitute A)
1 1/4 cups crumbled feta cheese

Blend the first four ingredients in a food processor or by hand until the mixture is smooth. Add the dip mix and cheese, and refrigerate the dip for at least 1 hour before serving.

Serves 4 to 6

ot Tomato Spread

This creamy, spicy spread, created by Sundance Foods of Bay View, Wisconsin, is as good to eat as it is colorful. Serve it on toasted pita wedges, crackers, or toasted flour tortillas.

1 1/4 cup tomato purée
1 to 4 tablespoons *Sundance Salsa Blend*
  (or substitute A)
Salt to taste
8 ounces light cream cheese, softened

In a small saucepan, bring the tomato purée and salsa blend to a boil. Add salt if you wish. Simmer the mixture for 10 minutes, then remove it from the heat and let it cool. Using a fork, blend the cream cheese and the tomato purée mixture. Chill the cream cheese mixture for 2 hours before serving.

Yields about 1 1/2 cups

arlic Tomato Spread

Clove 'n' Vine elephant garlic is truly flavorful. Diane Trenhaile, owner of Clove 'n' Vine, submitted this recipe. The spread is great on toast, fresh bread, or crackers; it also makes a good pasta sauce. Try adding herbs, such as parsley, rosemary, oregano, or basil.

2 heaping tablespoons *Clove 'n' Vine Dried Elephant Garlic Cloves* (or substitute other dried garlic cloves)
1 cup water
1/2 tablespoon minced dried tomatoes
1/4 cup olive oil
Cayenne powder to taste

Break up the garlic into small pieces. In a small saucepan, bring the water to a boil. Remove the pan from the heat, add the garlic, and allow it to reconstitute (this takes approximately 5 minutes). Drain the garlic when it is soft and plump. Add the dried tomatoes. Cover the mixture with the olive oil, sprinkle with cayenne, and serve it immediately.

Serves 2 to 4

tomic Shrimp Cocktail

Jeff Williams, the owner of Atomic Bob's, has created this spicy dish to tantalize the chile lover in you. The combination of flavors creates a mouthwatering experience for any barbecue fan.

3 pounds medium fresh shrimp
2 tablespoons butter
1/4 cup chopped green onions
2 garlic cloves, minced
1 tablespoon black pepper, coarsely ground
1/4 cup *Atomic Bob's Barbeque Sauce* (or substitute F)

Peel and devein the shrimp. Melt the butter in a large skillet and sauté the shrimp with the green onions and garlic until the shrimp is translucent. Add the black pepper and the barbecue sauce and simmer for 5 minutes.

Serve the shrimp alone as an hors d'oeuvre, or over rice as a main dish.

Serves 6

Trinidad Pepper Sauce and Cream Cheese Roll

Mary Jane Barnes of Caribbean Food Products has created this quick and easy empanada-style appetizer using her fine Trinidad Pepper Sauce. She imports the sauce from its creator, her mother, a longtime resident of Trinidad and Tobago, West Indies.

1 package unbaked crescent rolls

8 ounces cream cheese

1 medium ripe tomato, chopped

1 medium onion, chopped

1/3 cup *Trinidad Pepper Sauce* (or substitute G)

1/2 cup shredded Swiss cheese

1/2 cup butter, melted

Preheat the oven to 350 degrees.

Open eight crescent rolls and position 4 pieces in a square. Pinch together the pieces of dough, to make one solid bottom for the roll. Do the same to make the top. Flatten the cream cheese to 1/2 inch thick. Place the cream cheese in the center of the bottom square, and cover the cheese with the tomato, onion and pepper sauce. Top with the shredded cheese. Place the top square of dough over all of the ingredients, and pinch the edges together. Brush the top with the melted butter. Place the roll on a cookie sheet, and bake it for 15 to 20 minutes, or until it is golden brown.

Remove the roll from the oven, and let it cool for 15 to 20 minutes. Serve it on a platter accompanied by crisp raw vegetables.

Note: You can use a cookie cutter to make attractive individual pastries for any occasion.

Serves 4 to 6

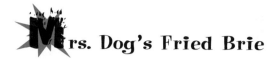

Mrs. Dog's Fried Brie

Mrs. Dog's has created this tasty brie recipe using her company's incredible mustard to add a tangy twist to a very buttery cheese. The contrast is perfect.

2 tablespoons Mrs. Dog's Mustard
  (or substitute H)
1 egg
2 tablespoons water
1 8-ounce round brie cheese
1/2 cup dried bread crumbs
2 tablespoons butter
1 pound French bread, cut into large cubes

In a pie plate, beat 1 teaspoon mustard with the egg and water until the mixture is foamy. Spread the bread crumbs on another plate. Spread the remaining mustard on the cheese, coating the entire surface. Dip the cheese into the egg mixture, then into the crumbs, coating the cheese well.

Heat the butter in a skillet until it is foamy. Add the brie, cover the skillet, and cook over low heat for 5 minutes. Turn the brie over, cover the skillet again, and cook until the brie is golden brown, about 5-10 minutes. Place the brie on a serving dish, and serve immediately with bread cubes. The bread cubes are dipped into the brie.

Serves 2 to 4

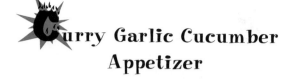

Curry Garlic Cucumber Appetizer

Since this treat requires a little advance preparation, you'll be glad to know that it is a real crowd-pleaser. Richard Reiher of the Virgin Islands Herb and Pepper Company has created this tasty combination of flavors.

1 large cucumber
1 cup cream cheese
1/4 cup Virgin Islands Herb and Pepper
  Company's Curry Garlic Sauce
  (or substitute I)

Cut off the ends of the cucumber, slice it in half lengthwise, and hollow out the center, removing the seeds but leaving the flesh. Mix the cream cheese and sauce together and fill the hollowed cucumber halves. Refrigerate the stuffed cucumber overnight before serving.

Serves 2 to 4

Caribbean Habanero Con Queso

Bob Kennedy of the Virgin Fire Company has devised this quick and easy cheese dip with a Caribbean flair. For a tasty variation, add chopped green onion, bell pepper, or other vegetables.

1 pound American cheese, cubed
1 1/3 cup canned cheddar cheese soup
1/4 cup *Virgin Fire Eastern Caribbean Hot Pepper Sauce* (or substitute G)

Combine all ingredients in a crock pot. Heat the mixture slowly until the cheese has completely melted. Serve with chips, or ladle the mixture over raw or steamed vegetables.

Serves 6 to 8

Paradise Pineapple and Shrimp Quesadillas

Goldwater's Foods of Arizona, a family-run business, offers this easy recipe for a great blend of flavors. For variety, try using crab or chicken in place of the shrimp. The pineapple in the salsa adds a taste of the tropics.

12 to 18 cooked medium shrimp, sliced lengthwise
6 8-inch flour or (white or whole wheat) tortillas
1 pound cheddar or jack cheese, shredded
1 small avocado, diced
1/4 cup chopped cilantro
1 jar *Goldwater's Paradise Pineapple Salsa* (or substitute J)

On one-half of each tortilla, layer the shrimp, cheese, avocado, and cilantro. Moisten the edges of the tortilla with water, and fold the tortilla in half. Press the edges together to seal them. Grill the quesadilla on both sides until the cheese is melted. Cut the quesadilla into wedges, and serve it with a generous helping of salsa.

Serves 6

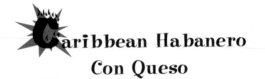

The Brown Adobe
The New Mexican Company
Chile Oil Olé

incronizadas

This recipe is a natural for family assembly-line preparation. The sincronizadas are tasty and filling and make a great brunch or lunch treat. Thank you to McIlhenny Company and Barbara Hunter for giving us this recipe.

2 tablespoons *Tabasco Jalapeño Sauce*
  (or substitute D)
12 flour tortillas
6 thin slices ham
2 cups grated jack cheese
2 ripe avocados, sliced
6 tablespoons chopped tomato
2 tablespoons chopped cilantro

Spread 1/2 teaspoon sauce on one side of each tortilla. For each sincronizada, place one tortilla, sauce side up, on a flat surface; add a slice of the ham; sprinkle with 2 1/2 tablespoons of the cheese, and arrange 3 slices of the avocado, 1 tablespoon of the chopped tomato, and 1 teaspoon of the cilantro over the ham. Distribute 2 1/2 additional tablespoons of cheese over the cilantro. Top with another tortilla, sauce side down, forming a tortilla sandwich (sincronizada). Set the sandwich aside, and repeat the process with the remaining tortillas and ingredients.

On a griddle or in a dry medium skillet, cook the sincronizadas one at a time over medium heat until they are crisp and lightly browned on each side and the cheese is melted. Cut the sincronizadas into wedges and serve them with your favorite dipping sauce. Or, serve them whole for a lunch or brunch entrée.

Serves 6

ensational Nachos

These are quick, easy, delicious, and the perfect snack for unexpected guests. Julienne Brown of the Brown Adobe may live in Pennsylvania, but don't let that fool you; her roots are in the heat heartland, New Mexico.

1-pound bag tortilla chips
1 jar *The Brown Adobe Salsa*
  (or substitute B)
1 1/2 cups cheddar or jack cheese
  (or both), grated
1/2 cup black olives, chopped
1/4 cup sour cream or guacamole
  (or both)

Preheat a broiler.

On an ovenproof platter, arrange the tortilla chips. Top with salsa and grated cheese. Broil the nachos until the cheese bubbles. Remove the platter from the oven and top the nachos with chopped black olives and dabs of sour cream, guacamole, or both.

Serves: 4

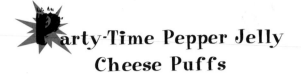

Party-Time Pepper Jelly Cheese Puffs

Just about any good pepper jelly can be used in this recipe, but we recommend Uncle Vinnie's or My Godfather's, both from Sumptuous Selections.

1/2 pound sharp cheddar cheese, grated
6 tablespoons butter, chilled and cut into
  small pieces
1 cup all-purpose flour
1/2 jar *Uncle Vinnie's Hot Pepper Jelly* or
  My Godfather's Sweet Pepper Jelly

Combine the cheese, butter, and flour in a food processor, pulsing 1 second at a time until the mixture resembles coarse meal. Then let the processor run about 5 to 6 seconds, until the dough forms a ball (or use two knives or a pastry blender to cut the flour into the cheese and butter). Don't overwork the dough. Wrap the dough in plastic; chill it for 30 minutes.

Preheat the oven to 400 degrees. Working quickly, roll the dough into 1-inch balls (dampen your hands with cold water if the dough becomes too sticky). Place the balls 1 inch apart on an ungreased cookie sheet. Bake 5 minutes. Remove the sheet from the oven, and with your thumb form a small depression in the top of each puff. Fill each with a dollop of pepper jelly. Return the sheet to the oven and cook the puffs just until they are golden brown.

Yields about 40 hors d'oeuvres

Crispy Fried Won Tons

These won tons from Century Sauce Kitchens are the perfect appetizer to serve before an Asian meal. We recommend frying them in canola oil.

3 chicken thighs, skinned and deboned
6 tablespoons *Century Hot Pepper Sauce*
  (or substitute D)
1 tablespoon grated fresh ginger
4 green onions, minced
1 teaspoon sesame oil
1 teaspoon soy sauce
1 package won ton wrappers
Vegetable oil, for deep frying

Dipping sauce:
1/4 cup *Century Hot Pepper Sauce*
  (or substitute D)
1/4 cup soy sauce

Grind together the first six ingredients in a food processor, taking care not to purée them. Place approximately 1/2 teaspoon filling in each won ton wrapper, moisten the edges of the wrapper with water, and fold the wrapper according to the package directions, pressing out any trapped air.

Heat the oil. Deep-fry the won tons, a few at a time, until they are brown and crisp, and drain them on paper towels.

To make the dipping sauce, combine the hot pepper sauce and soy sauce, and mix well. Serve the won tons hot, accompanied by the sauce.

Yields 50 won tons

Tortilla Cream Cheese Roll-Ups

Greg Dineen of Santa Fe Seasons created this appetizer, using some of his company's fine products. These tasty, easy-to-make roll-ups are perfect for a party because they can be made ahead of time. If you or your guests are watching fat intake, use low-fat cream cheese.

8 ounces cream cheese
1/4 cup *Santa Fe Seasons Red Chile Salsa*
  (or substitute B)
1/2 teaspoon *Santa Fe Season's Chile Blend*
  (or substitute A)
1/4 cup chopped mushrooms
6 to 8 flour tortillas
3/4 cup sliced black olives
1 1/2 bunches spinach
1 bunch green onions, roots cut off

Beat together the cream cheese, red chile salsa, chile blend, and mushrooms until the mixture is light and fluffy. Place 3 tablespoons of the mixture on each tortilla and spread it evenly, leaving a 1-inch margin on opposite sides. Divide the olives among the tortillas, and cover with the whole spinach leaves. Place the whole green stock of a green onion across each tortilla. Roll the tortilla tightly, starting from a bare edge; use the remaining cream cheese to help hold the roll together. Put the tortillas on a plate and cover them with plastic. Refrigerate the rolls overnight.

Let the rolls stand for 10 minutes at room temperature, then slice them crosswise into approximately 8 pieces. Serve them immediately.

Serves 8 to 10

Tropical Style Buffalo Wings

Theresa O'Hara of St. Thomas, Virgin Islands, is the creator of Heat Wave Hot Sauce and these spicy buffalo wings. They are a good choice to serve at a large party, since all the preparation can be done ahead of time.

1 1/4 cups *Heat Wave Northside Hot Sauce* (or substitute **G**)
2 1/2 cups barbecue sauce
1/2 pound butter or margarine
1/4 cup granulated garlic
3 tablespoons *Tabasco Pepper Sauce* (or substitute **D**)
Vegetable oil, for deep frying
2 to 3 pounds chicken wings

In a saucepan, bring the first five ingredients to a boil. Set the sauce aside.

Heat the oil. Deep-fry the chicken wings, a few at a time, until they are crisp. When the wings are all cooked, toss them with the sauce in a nonreactive bowl. Place the coated wings on a serving platter, and serve them warm. (They can be kept warm in the oven, but take care that they don't dry out.)

Serves 6 to 8

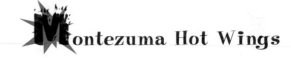

Montezuma Hot Wings

Montezuma sauces created by Chuck Evans of Sauces and Salsas Ltd. have been heating up Ohio for many years. These wings are really hot and spicy. The process of baking and then frying the wings gives better results than either baking or deep-frying alone.

3 to 5 pounds chicken wings
Corn oil, for deep-frying
1 16-ounce jar *Karen's Hot Wings Sauce* (or, for even hotter wings, *Montezuma Habanero Hot Wings Sauce*) (or substitute **G**)
Celery sticks
Blue cheese or ranch dressing

Preheat the oven to 350 degrees.

Break each wing at the outer joint, and remove and discard the wing tip. Place the chicken wings in a shallow baking pan, and bake them for about 30 to 40 minutes, or until they are done. Heat the corn oil in a large saucepan over medium-high heat. Put the baked wings, a handful at a time, into the saucepan, and fry them until the skin turns light brown. Serve them with a bowl of the hot sauce (or put the finished wings and sauce into a closed container, and shake until the wings are well coated). Accompany the dish with celery sticks and blue cheese or ranch dressing, to take some of the sting out of the hot wings.

Serves 6 to 8

ango Honey-Mustard Wings

Isla Vieques Condiment Company of Puerto Rico devised this spicy, tropical recipe for chicken wings; the taste is a delicious blend of heat, mangos, and honey.

2 pounds chicken wings
Vegetable oil, for deep frying
Lettuce leaves, for garnish
1 carrot, grated, for garnish
1/2 cup *Isla Vieques Jalapeño Mango Mustard* (or substitute H)
1/4 cup *Isla Vieques Hot 'n' Honey Hot Sauce* (or substitute G)
1/3 cup brown sugar

Remove the wing tips, and discard them. Deep-fry the chicken wings in the vegetable oil until they are golden brown. Keep the wings warm.

Spread the lettuce leaves on a serving plate, and sprinkle the grated carrot over the lettuce.

Combine the mustard, hot sauce, and brown sugar in a saucepan large enough to hold all the wings, and heat the mixture until it is bubbly. Add the wings to the saucepan, and mix until the wings are completely coated with the sauce. Place the wings on top of the lettuce, and serve them hot as an appetizer.

Serves 4

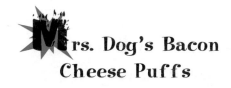rs. Dog's Bacon Cheese Puffs

Mrs. Dog's Products have been adding spice to the lives of the people in Michigan for many years. This dish is very easy to prepare, and because of the unique mustard, the taste is at once spicy and sweet.

8 to 12 slices bacon
1/4 cup *Mrs. Dog's Mustard*
1 cup grated Swiss cheese
4 to 6 thin slices of bread

Preheat the oven to 400 degrees.

Cut the bacon crosswise into 3-inch pieces, and lightly coat one side of each piece with mustard. Sprinkle the slices amply with the cheese, saving a small amount for later. Cut the bread slices into 4-inch squares, trimming off the crusts. Lay a piece of bread over each slice of bacon, and roll the bread and bacon together. Secure the rolls with toothpicks and place the rolls in a shallow pan. Sprinkle the remaining cheese on top of them. Bake the rolls for 20 minutes, then serve them immediately.

Serves 4 to 6

Vegetarian Burritos with Spicy Bean Sauce

Thank you to Diana and Jim Starke of Isla Vieques for this unusual burrito recipe with such an interesting combination of flavors. These burritos would make a great appetizer.

1 medium onion, chopped

4 garlic cloves, minced

2 tablespoons minced cilantro

2 tablespoons vegetable oil

2 cubanelle peppers or one bell pepper, chopped

1 cup diced broccoli

1 cup grated cheddar or jack cheese

4 10-inch flour tortillas

2 cups cooked kidney beans, drained and rinsed

1 cup tomato sauce

1/4 cup *Isla Vieques Salsa Picante* (or substitute **B**)

1/4 cup water

Preheat the oven to 375 degrees.

Set aside a quarter of the onion, half the garlic, and half the cilantro. Heat the oil in a skillet, and sauté together the remaining onion, garlic, and cilantro, the peppers, and the broccoli until the broccoli is barely tender. Place one quarter of this mixture and 1 tablespoon grated cheese in each tortilla, and roll the tortilla, tucking in the ends. Arrange the rolled tortillas in a casserole dish.

In a blender, purée the beans, tomato sauce, salsa, water, and the reserved onion, garlic, and cilantro. Pour this mixture over the tortillas, top with the remaining cheese, and bake the burritos for 30 minutes.

Serve the burritos hot.

Serves 2 as a main course, 4 as an appetizer

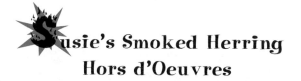

Susie's Smoked Herring Hors d'Oeuvres

Rosemarie McMaster's hot sauce, Susie's, comes from the lovely Caribbean island of Antigua, where hot sauce and fish are frequently paired. Rosemarie's excellent appetizer is a taste of the tropics.

I pound skinless smoked herring
1/2 cup vegetable oil
2 green onions, diced
I each red, green, and yellow medium bell peppers, diced
3 garlic cloves, crushed
2 sprigs fresh thyme, or 2 teaspoons dried
I medium onion, finely chopped
1/2 teaspoon honey
1/4 cup *Susie's Hot Sauce* (or substitute G)

Pour hot water over the herring and soak it for about 45 minutes.

Drain the herring and flake it, removing as many bones as possible.

Heat the oil over low heat, and add the green onions, bell peppers, garlic, thyme, and onions. Sauté the mixture for about 3 minutes. Add the honey, stir it in, and pour the mixture over the fish. Add the hot sauce, and mix well. Chill the mixture. Serve the herring with crackers, chips, or toast.

Serves 2 to 4

Sassy Sauces, Salads, and Soups

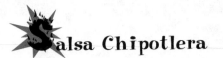

Salsa Chipotlera

This salsa from Chile Bravo! Imports uses those wonderful smoky chiles—the chipotles. The salsa complements all kinds of meat and can also be used as a dip.

2 *Avante Chipotle Chiles*
3 tablespoons Avante liquid
1 bunch parsley, minced
1 bunch cilantro, minced
2 tablespoons oregano
1 teaspoon salt
1 cup olive oil
1/2 cup vinegar

Blend all the ingredients and refrigerate the mixture for 24 hours.

Use the salsa to top cuts of beef, lamb, or pork; fajitas; or a chicken dish.

Yields 3 to 4 cups

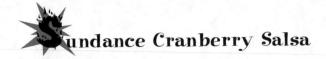

Sundance Cranberry Salsa

Serve this Sundance dish with grilled or roasted fish, poultry, or meat. The interesting combination of fruit and spice is a delight to the palate.

1 tablespoon canola oil
1 medium onion, chopped
12 ounces fresh cranberries
1 medium apple, peeled, cored, and chopped
2 tablespoons dry *Sundance Salsa Blend* (or substitute A)
1 tablespoon vinegar
3 tablespoons sugar
1/4 cup water
1/4 teaspoon ground nutmeg
Salt and pepper to taste

Heat a medium saucepan and add the oil. When the oil is hot, add the onion, and sauté until it is soft, about 5 minutes. Add the cranberries, apple, salsa blend, vinegar, sugar, and water, and mix well. Heat the mixture over medium-low heat, covered. Cook, stirring occasionally, until the cranberries are soft, about 15 minutes. Do not let the mixture boil.

Stir in the nutmeg, salt, and pepper. Serve the salsa hot.

Yields 2 cups

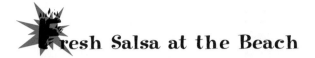resh Salsa at the Beach

This outstanding fresh-fruit salsa recipe was created by Chip Hearn, the owner of Peppers, a hot-sauce manufacturer. The taste is tropical with a kick. Eating this salsa is a great way to include more fruit in your diet. (By the way, Chip is not being sexist with the name of his hot sauce; he also manufactures a "male" sauce, Hot Buns at the Beach.)

1 pineapple, peeled, cored, and cut into 1/4-inch dice
2 mangos, peeled, pitted and cut into 1/4-inch dice
2 kiwis, peeled and cut into 1/4-inch dice
1/2 red bell pepper, finely diced
1 yellow bell pepper, finely diced
2 tablespoons finely diced red onion
1 tablespoon orange juice
1/2 tablespoon finely chopped cilantro
2 teaspoons grated fresh ginger
1 tablespoon light brown sugar
2 tablespoons *Hot Bitch at the Beach* (or substitute D)

Combine all the ingredients and chill the mixture.

This salsa is delicious with grilled fish, chicken, or pork. You might serve the salsa in the shell of half the orange you squeezed for juice.

Serves: 4 to 6

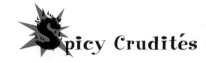picy Crudités

If your vegetables are fresh from the garden, this dish from GTL, Inc., will be even more delicious. It is good not only as crudités or as a dip, but also as a topping for grilled fish or chicken.

3 medium ripe tomatoes, chopped
2 cucumbers, seeded and chopped
1 green bell pepper, chopped
1 red onion, chopped
3 tablespoons *Pili Hot Pepper Condiment* (or substitute L)
Salt to taste

Combine the tomatoes, cucumbers, pepper, and onion. Stir in the Pili and salt, and marinate the mixture for at least 4 hours. Eat it on its own or serve it with corn chips.

Serves 6

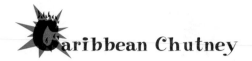 # Caribbean Chutney

From Sgt. Pepper's, based in Austin, Texas, comes this jazzy tropical recipe. Try the chutney with grilled meat, especially pork.

1/4 cup golden raisins
2 tablespoons dark rum
1/4 cup water
1/2 cup light brown sugar, firmly packed
1/2 cup diced yellow onion
1/2 cup *Salza Vinegar* (or substitute **C**)
1/4 cup balsalmic vinegar
1 tablespoon jerk seasoning (dry or paste)
1 juice and zest of 1 lime
2 mangos, peeled, seeded, and diced
1 tablespoon *Texas Tears Habanero Sauce*
   (or substitute **G**)
1 teaspoon minced fresh gingerroot
1 banana, diced

Soak the raisins in rum and enough hot water to cover them. In a saucepan, bring the water, sugar, onion, and vinegars to a boil. Add the jerk seasoning, lime juice, mangos, habanero sauce, and ginger. Lower the heat, and simmer the mixture for 30 minutes or until it thickens.

Stir in the raisins and banana. Chill the chutney until you're ready to serve it.

Serves 4

 # Tamarillo Chutney

Kiwi Dundee, in Albuquerque, imports prepared foods from Australia and New Zealand. Watch for tamarillos to become popular; known to the Incas, the fruits are now a new cash crop from down under.

2 pounds tamarillos, peeled and chopped
   (or substitute mangos)
1 pound onion, peeled and chopped
1 pound cooking apples, peeled and
   chopped
4 cups brown sugar
2 cups vinegar
1 tablespoon whole pickling spices
   (e.g., peppercorns or cloves)
1 teaspoon salt
1/4 to 1/2 teaspoon cayenne powder

Place all of the ingredients in a large, heavy pot and slowly bring the mixture to a boil. Reduce the heat, and simmer the mixture slowly for about 2 hours or until it is thick.

Pour the chutney into sterilized jars, and seal the jars.

Serve the chutney with hot and cold meats, pâtés, cheeses, and bread and crackers.

Serves 4 to 6

Pineapple Chutney

Jeanne Kyser's company, Spirit Mesa, is located in Tijeras, New Mexico, in the scenic Sandia Mountains. Serve this flavorful chutney with roasted turkey, smoked turkey, or grilled chicken.

1/2 fresh pineapple, peeled and cored
1/4 cup peeled and minced fresh ginger
1/8 cup minced lemon zest
1 1/2 cups light brown sugar
1 1/2 cups *Spirit Mesa Mint Vinegar*
  (or substitute C)
1 cup pitted and chopped dates
1/2 cup currants
1/2 teaspoon dried crushed red chile
1/4 teaspoon ground allspice
1/2 teaspoon salt

Cut the pineapple into 2/3-inch cubes (to make about 2 cups). Combine all of the ingredients in a heavy nonreactive saucepan, and bring the mixture to a boil over high heat. Lower the heat slightly, and boil until the chutney has thickened, about 1 hour. Transfer the mixture to sterilized jars, and store them in the refrigerator.

Yields about 4 to 6 cups

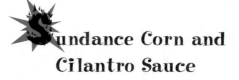

Sundance Corn and Cilantro Sauce

This interesting sauce from Sundance Foods is quite rich, with a kick from the dry salsa blend. Try the sauce with grilled meats or even over chile pasta.

1 to 1 1/4 cups heavy cream
1/4 cup water
2 tablespoons dry *Sundance Salsa Blend*
  (or substitute A)
2 cups fresh corn kernels (from 2 large
  or 4 small ears)
1 1/2 tablespoons chopped cilantro

Combine 1 cup of the cream, the water, and the salsa in a medium saucepan, and bring the mixture to a boil over medium heat. Reduce the heat, and simmer about 10 minutes, until the mixture is reduced to 1 cup. Add the corn, and continue simmering until the corn is tender, about 5 to 8 minutes. Transfer the mixture to a food processor or blender, and blend until the mixture is smooth. Strain the purée through a very fine sieve set over a clean saucepan (if you want a chunky sauce, pour it directly into the saucepan). Place the saucepan over medium heat, and simmer for 3 minutes to blend the flavors, adding more cream for a thinner consistency. Stir in the cilantro.

Serve the sauce immediately with grilled fish, chicken, or pork.

Yields 1 1/2 cups

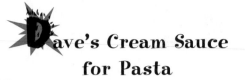

Dave's Cream Sauce for Pasta

Texas Tears Chicken Marinade

This recipe, from Dave's Gourmet, combines a creamy taste with the fiery heat of Dave's grilling sauce. We think this would even be good for a new twist on scalloped potatoes!

Sgt. Pepper's of Austin has created this easy, delicious marinade for chicken. If you are grilling outside, use a vegetable screen so the onion rings don't disappear through the grill.

I teaspoon vegetable oil
2 garlic cloves, minced
I medium bell pepper, diced
1/2 cup *Dave's Greatest Grilling Sauce*
   (or substitute M)
2 cups milk
4 ounces Parmesan cheese, shredded
Salt and pepper to taste

2 tablespoons *Texas Tears Habanero Sauce*
   (or substitute D)
I cup Italian dressing
I lime
1/2 bunch cilantro, chopped
I large onion, sliced into 1/4-inch rings

Heat the oil in a small saucepan. Add the garlic and bell pepper, and sauté them until the bell pepper is tender. Add the remaining ingredients, and simmer gently until the sauce thickens slightly. Serve it hot over pasta.

Combine all of the ingredients, and pour the marinade over a cut-up chicken. Marinate the chicken overnight. Grill or broil the chicken and the onion rings, and serve them at once.

Yields 2 cups

Serves 4 to 6

callop Sauce for Fish

Caribbean Food Products presents a seafood extrava-ganza in this recipe. What a double whammy! Here described as a topping for fish, the scallop sauce is equally delicious over pasta; we suggest a chile pasta for an extra wallop of flavor.

1 pound fresh scallops
1/3 cup *Trinidad Pepper Sauce*
  (or substitute G)
1 tablespoon lime juice
1/2 cup chopped green onions
4 teaspoons olive oil
1/2 cup tequila
1 cup Italian tomatoes, puréed
2 teaspoons capers
2 teaspoons chopped parsley
2 teaspoons butter
3/4 cup feta or other cheese

Marinate the scallops in the 1/3 cup Trinidad Pepper Sauce and lime juice for 30 minutes.

In a frying pan over medium heat, sauté the green onions in the olive oil for 3 to 4 minutes. Add the tequila, tomatoes, capers, and parsley, and bring the mixture to a boil. Reduce the heat, and simmer the sauce for 10–15 minutes.

Drain the marinade from the scallops. In a frying pan, melt the butter. Sauté the scallops, then add them to the sauce.

Spoon the hot sauce over broiled or baked fish fillets, top with the cheese, and broil the fish for an additional 3 minutes.

Serves 2

Gator Tail Sauce

Produced by Gator Hammock, the fiery Gator Sauce is not to be taken lightly! Gator Tail Sauce is great served with shrimp, oysters, and other seafood. And, of course, fried gator tail.

2 cups ketchup
3 tablespoons Gator Sauce
  (or substitute D)
2 tablespoons grated horseradish
2 teaspoons key lime juice

Mix all the ingredients, and chill the sauce for at least 3 hours before serving.

Yields 2 1/2 cups

Mahan's Southwest Gourmet Ribs

From Robert Mahan, the beret-sporting owner of Mahan's Southwest Gourmet Sauce, comes this tasty recipe for beef or pork. Boiling the meat before grilling it not only removes the excess fat, but also keeps the meat from charring on the grill before it is fully cooked.

2 pounds beef or pork ribs
1/2 cup chopped celery
1/2 cup chopped onion
2 chopped garlic cloves
Salt, pepper, and onion and garlic powders
  to taste
2 cups Mahan's Southwest Gourmet
  Marinade Sauce (or substitute M)

Add to a large pot of boiling water the ribs, celery, onion, and garlic. Parboil the meat and vegetables for 35 minutes. Remove the ribs, drain them, and pat them dry. Season the ribs with salt, pepper, garlic powder, and onion powder.

To bake the ribs, place them in a baking dish; pour the sauce over the meat. Cook until the meat is tender.

To broil, grill, or smoke the ribs, spray them first with sweet vermouth. Five minutes before the meat is done, brush them on both sides with the sauce.

Serve the ribs hot.

Serves 4

atay Marinade

The manufacturer of Pure Hell Hot Sauce, Andrew Hahn of Two Chefs, has given us this very interesting recipe. It was designed to be used in Asian grilled meats or satays. Try the marinade on meat, tofu, or stir-fry, or use it to spice up a salad and really surprise your guests!

1/4 cup minced cilantro

1 cup soy sauce

1/4 cup brown sugar

1/2 cup minced onions

1/2 cup lemon juice

4 small garlic cloves, crushed

1/4 cup ground coriander

2 tablespoons ground black pepper

1 teaspoon cayenne

1/4 cup ground Brazil nuts

1 cup olive oil

1 tablespoon *Pure Hell Hot Sauce*
  (or substitute G)

Combine all of the ingredients in a glass jar, and shake it to mix them thoroughly. Allow the marinade to sit for several hours refrigerated and then shake it again before using it.

Yields 3 1/2 to 4 cups

ut and Honey Glaze

Chef Eddie Adams offers this unusual, delicious glaze for meats, using one of his products, Eddie's Cajun Flavors Meat Spice. The citrus contrasts nicely with the nuts and the meat spice. If you are ever in Albuquerque, be sure to eat at Eddie's restaurant, The Gulf Coast Eatery.

5 tablespoons butter

3/4 cup diced onion

3/4 cup diced celery

1 cup nuts, chopped, or slivered pine,
  macadamia, or almonds

2 tablespoons *Eddie's Cajun Flavors Meat Spice* **(or substitute N)**

1 cup honey

1 teaspoon citrus (lemon, orange,
  or lime) peel

1 cup chicken broth or water

In a large skillet, melt 3 tablespoons butter over high heat. Sauté the celery and onions for 2 minutes or until they are tender. Add the nuts and meat spice, and stir well for 4 to 5 minutes. Add the honey, stirring again for 1 minute. Add the citrus peel and chicken stock, and stir well. Whisk until the sauce thickens, then remove the mixture from the heat. Let it stand for 5 to 10 minutes before using it.

Generously brush some of the glaze onto the meat 1 to 2 minutes before it's ready to come off the grill. Reserve the remaining glaze for dipping.

Yields 3 to 4 cups

Blackberry Barbecue Sauce

This interesting barbecue sauce, created by the Two Chefs company, is excellent on chicken, baby-back ribs, and brisket. Cook the meat and sauce slowly in a crock pot, so the fruit and heat will permeate the meat and make it very tender. The recipe can be halved.

3 pints puréed blackberries
1/4 cup Chambord liqueur
I quart beef broth
I quart tomato sauce
1/4 cup barbecue sauce
2 tablespoons *Pure Hell Hot Sauce*
  (or substitute G)
I teaspoon ground allspice
2 teaspoons onion powder
I 1/2 tablespoons cayenne pepper
1/2 teaspoon ground star anise
I small onion, minced

In a large saucepan, combine all the ingredients. Bring them to a boil, reduce the heat, and simmer the sauce uncovered for approximately 20 minutes. Remove from the heat and strain.

Yields 12 cups

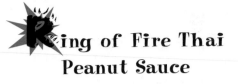

Ring of Fire Thai Peanut Sauce

This recipe from the Ring of Fire Hot Sauce company puts a new twist on a traditional Thai sauce. Take advantage of the wide range of Oriental vegetables available to add crunch and variety to the stir-fry.

1/4 cup light soy sauce or low-sodium
  soy sauce
1/2 cup water
1/4 cup honey
2 tablespoons peanut butter, preferably
  chunky
I tablespoon brown sugar
I 1/2 tablespoons *Ring of Fire Hot Sauce*
  (or substitute G)
1/2 teaspoon sesame oil

In a small bowl, whisk together the soy sauce, water, and honey.

In a skillet, melt the peanut butter. Slowly whisk in the soy sauce mixture; continue whisking until the mixture is smooth. Add the brown sugar, hot sauce, and sesame oil. Simmer the sauce 3 to 5 minutes. Remove the pan from the heat.

Stir-fry vegetables and meat or seafood of your choice. About 2 minutes before the meat and vegetables are fully cooked, stir in the sauce. Serve the mixture over noodles or rice.

Yields 3 1/4 cups

 ## reamy Tomato Salad Mold

The Chugwater Chili Company of Chugwater, Wyoming, has created this refreshing, spicy mold that is perfect to serve as a luncheon entrée on those sweltering days of summer. Serve the mold on a bed of mixed greens. It is made with their chili con carne mix.

1 to 2 teaspoons *Chugwater Chili Mix*
6 ounces cream cheese
1 1/4 cups canned tomato soup
2 packages unflavored gelatin
1/3 cup cold water
1 cup mayonnaise
1 cup finely diced celery
1/2 cup finely diced green onion
1 cup finely diced green pepper
1 cup cooked small shrimp

In a saucepan over low heat, combine the chili mix, cream cheese, and soup.

Dissolve the gelatin in the cold water, and add the gelatin solution to the soup mixture. Mix well, remove the pan from the heat, and let the mixture cool.

Add the mayonnaise, vegetables, and shrimp to the mixture. Pour the mixture into a 2-quart mold, rinsed in cold water, and chill the mold at least 4 hours.

Before serving, unmold the mold onto a chilled plate.

Serves 6

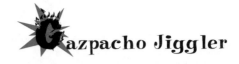 ## azpacho Jiggler

From Southwest Seasons comes this interesting gelatin recipe. Serve "the jiggler" on Bibb lettuce and endive.

2 cups chopped tomatoes
1/2 cup chopped green chile
1/2 cup chopped celery
1/2 cup chopped onion
2 tablespoons chopped parsley
1 1/2 teaspoons salt
1/4 teaspoon ground black pepper
2 tablespoons tarragon vinegar
Dash Worcestershire sauce
1 6-ounce package lemon gelatin
2 cups boiling water
1 1/2 cups cold water

Combine the vegetables, seasonings, vinegar, and Worcestershire sauce in a bowl.

In a mold, dissolve the gelatin in the boiling water. Add the cold water. Chill the mixture until it starts to set. Stir in the vegetable mixture, and chill the jiggler at least 4 hours.

Yields 5 cups

Serves 6 to 8

Ensalada Nuevo Mexicana

From W.C. Longacre, the owner of W.C.'s Mountain Road Café and a headliner at the cooking demonstrations at the Fiery Foods Show, comes this unique salad that needs no dressing. At the café, he says, "We offer eight salads daily—this is the most popular."

Mixed greens, such as romaine lettuce,
   butter lettuce, and torn spinach
1 hard-boiled egg, peeled and sliced
1/4 cup canned or fresh New Mexican
   chile strips
1 boned and skinned chicken breast,
   marinated in teriyaki sauce and grilled,
   then cut into 6 long, thin pieces
2 tablespoons guacamole
1 tablespoon salsa of your choice
3 tortilla chips
2 tablespoons cooked garbanzo beans
1 tablespoon chopped green onions
2 tablespoons diced tomatoes
Grated cheddar cheese, for garnish
   (optional)

Place the greens on a plate, top them with the egg slices. Place first half the chile strips, next half the chicken strips, then the remaining chile strips and finally the remaining chicken strips alternately on top of the egg slices. Scoop the guacamole onto the top, and spoon the salsa over the guacamole. Crown the dish with the 3 tortilla chips, stick into the guacamole. Sprinkle the salad with the beans, onions, and tomatoes, and garnish, if you like, with the cheese.

Serves: 1

Tex-Mex Slaw

Sundance provided us with this recipe; it is a great change from the usual mayonnaise-laden slaws.

I large head cabbage, thinly sliced
2 medium Spanish onions, thinly sliced
I red bell pepper, thinly sliced
I cup plus 2 tablespoons sugar
I cup vinegar
I cup canola oil
2 tablespoons *Sundance All-Purpose Southwest Seasoning* (or substitute **A**)
I tablespoon *Sundance Salsa Blend* (or substitute **A**)
I tablespoon dry mustard
Salt to taste

Mix the cabbage, onions, pepper, and I cup sugar in a large bowl, and set the bowl aside.

Put the remaining ingredients into a saucepan, and bring them to a boil. Remove the pan from the heat and pour the dressing over the cabbage mixture. Toss to blend the flavors. Refrigerate the slaw in an airtight container. It will improve with age for as long as several weeks.

Yields 3 quarts

Pat's Spring Mint Salad

Spirit Mesa contributed this recipe for an exotic-tasting, crunchy salad. Serve it with grilled shrimp, basted with a little butter and fresh lime juice.

1/2 cup sugar
1/4 cup sliced almonds
I cup plain nonfat yogurt
Spirit Mesa Mint Vinegar to taste (or substitute **C**)
Assorted salad greens
I tangerine, peeled and segmented
1/2 cup chopped celery
1/4 cup slivered jicama
1/4 cup minced mint
I teaspoon grated fresh ginger
Salt and pepper to taste

Caramelize the sugar by melting it in a heavy skillet over low heat. Add 2 tablespoons of the sliced almonds to the melted sugar, stirring constantly till they are coated. Spread them on buttered waxed paper to cool, and then break them apart.

Mix I cup of the yogurt with enough Spirit Mesa Mint Vinegar to make a dressing of medium consistency.

Tear the salad greens, and put them into a serving bowl with the tangerine, celery, jicama and mint. Pour the dressing over the salad mixture. Top with the caramelized almonds, ginger, and salt and pepper. Toss the salad, and serve it immediately, garnished with the remaining almonds.

Serves 4 to 6

Chinese Chicken Salad

Wayne Doerr of the Alder Market is the creator of some fine salad dressings. This tasty dish takes only a few minutes to make. It's wonderful with this red vinegar dressing.

4 ounces Chinese rice sticks
2 tablespoons vegetable oil
3/4 *Alder Spinach Salad Dressing*
1/4 teaspoon cayenne powder
4 teaspoons sesame oil
2 tablespoons sliced green onions
1/2 teaspoon minced fresh gingerroot
4 teaspoons soy sauce
2 boned chicken breast halves
8 ounces greens and flowers salad mix
1/2 cup mandarin orange segments
1 tablespoon cilantro leaves
1/2 cup chopped almonds

Fry the rice sticks in hot oil, and drain them on paper towels.

In a small bowl, mix the salad dressing, cayenne, sesame oil, green onions, ginger, and soy sauce.

Grill the chicken breasts. Slice the breasts, put the slices into a bowl, and toss them with one-third of the dressing.

Divide the rice sticks among four salad plates. In a large bowl, toss the salad mix with the mandarin oranges and fresh cilantro leaves. Add the remaining dressing, toss the salad mix again, and mound it on the rice sticks. Top each plate with some of the chicken slices and sprinkle with the almonds.

Serves 4

Tamarillo and Mushroom Salad with Honey Dressing

Like other ingredients with powerful flavors, such as onions, chiles, and lemons, tamarillos enhance and complement a vast range of other foods. In this recipe, tamarillos are added for flavor and color. We thank Mary Jo Honeycutt and Robert Vigil of Kiwi Dundee for the recipe.

4 to 6 lettuce leaves
1 1/2 cups button mushrooms
3 tamarillos, blanched, peeled, and sliced
   (or substitute mangos)
1/2 teaspoon cayenne powder
Freshly ground black pepper
2 tablespoons honey
1/4 cup red wine vinegar
1/4 cup vegetable oil

Divide the lettuce leaves among salad plates, top with the mushrooms and tamarillo slices. Sprinkle with the cayenne and pepper. Combine the remaining ingredients and spoon the dressing over the salad just before serving.

Serves 4 to 6

Sandy Spivey's Pasta Salad

Dale Lucas of the G. L. Mezzetta company offers this salad recipe that is rich with the taste of two cheeses and fresh basil. Basil is easy to grow, and every cook should have it available fresh in season.

1 pound pasta shells
2 cups *Mezzetta Roasted Red Peppers*,
   sliced thin (or substitute red bell
   peppers, roasted)
2 cups fresh basil leaves, torn into
   small pieces
2 cups shredded Mozzarella cheese
1 cup shredded Romano cheese
1 1/4 cups toasted walnut pieces
2 medium garlic cloves, crushed
1 1/2 tablespoons dried red pepper flakes
1/4 cup lemon juice
Salt and pepper to taste

Cook the pasta shells according to the package directions. Rinse the pasta with cold water and drain the pasta well.

Put the pasta and the Red Peppers, basil, cheeses, and walnuts in a large bowl, and mix them. Put the remaining ingredients in a small mixing bowl, and whisk well until they are blended. Pour the dressing over the pasta mixture, toss well, and serve.

Serves 4

Chicken Tortellini Salad

We thank the Alder Market for this recipe. The combination of black olives, walnuts, and the Alder vinaigrette make a wonderfully tasty salad. Try it chilled or at room temperature.

2 cups uncooked tortellini
2 cups cooked and cubed chicken meat
2 cups drained water-packed
  artichoke hearts
2 small tomatoes, diced
1 cup black olives, sliced
1 cup walnuts, chopped
Alder Market Mustard Vinaigrette to taste
  (or substitute equal parts **C** and **H**)

Cook and drain the pasta. Put it into a serving bowl. Add the remaining ingredients and toss lightly to coat everything with the vinaigrette. Serve the salad at room temperature, or chill it before serving.

Serves 8 to 10

Icy Spicy Tomato Soup

Isla Vieques Company of Puerto Rico created this recipe using some of their fine products. The taste of the vegetables is enlivened with the fresh basil, the vinegar, and the salsa.

6 medium tomatoes, chopped
1 cucumber, peeled, seeded, and chopped
1/2 small onion, chopped
1 garlic clove, minced
10 fresh basil leaves
1/4 cup red wine vinegar
2 tablespoons *Isla Vieques Salsa Picante*
  (or substitute **B**)
1/2 cup olive oil
1 1/2 cups soft bread crumbs
3/4 cup ice water

Combine the ingredients. Purée them in two batches in a blender. Chill the soup until serving time.

Serve the soup with garlic toast.

Serves 6

 erk Chicken Salad

The Busha Browne Company of Jamaica has given us this recipe; it is a new use for a traditional Jamaican seasoning—jerk. The flavors in jerk seasoning are strong, pungent, and spicy. In Jamaica, your nose will lead you to the nearest "jerk shack."

Great House Vinaigrette Dressing:

2 garlic cloves, crushed

1/2 cup herb vinegar

1/2 cup dry red wine

1 tablespoon *Busha Browne's Spicy and Hot Pepper Sherry* (or substitute Q)

2 tablespoons sugar

1/2 teaspoon celery salt

1 teaspoon dried oregano

1/4 teaspoon freshly ground black pepper

1 cup olive oil

The Salad:

2 tablespoons *Busha Browne's Jerk Seasoning* (or substitute Q)

1/2 cup olive oil

4 whole chicken breasts, split, boned, and trimmed

4 medium onions, julienne

1 sweet red pepper, cut into strips

1 green bell pepper, cut into strips

1 cup mung bean sprouts

1/4 cup chopped parsley

3 black olives, slivered (optional)

For the dressing: Soak the crushed garlic in the herb vinegar and red wine. Stir in the remaining ingredients, adding the olive oil last. Pour this mixture into a glass jar, and shake well. The dressing does not require refrigeration.

Mix together the jerk seasoning and 1/4 cup olive oil, and brush it on the chicken breasts. Allow the breasts to marinate (covered and refrigerated) for at least 1 hour.

Preheat the oven to 325 degrees.

Lay the chicken breast halves flat in a roasting pan, cover the pan with foil, and cook the chicken in the oven for 10 minutes or until it is done. Let the chicken cool, then cut it into bite-size strips and refrigerate it.

Heat the remaining olive oil in a frying pan.

Sauté the onions, peppers, and bean sprouts in batches. Let the sautéed vegetables cool, then mix them together in a bowl with the chicken, parsley, and black olives. Refrigerate the salad.

When all the ingredients have chilled, pour the dressing over the chicken mixture, and toss the salad lightly but thoroughly. Serve it with tomatoes and salad greens.

Serves 4

Spicy Zucchini Soup

Tom Hill of Chef's Choice, the creator of Whiplash Sauce, gives us one very good way to eat our vegetables! The blend of the spicy sauce and the cream cheese is very smooth on the tongue.

2 cups chopped onion
3 garlic cloves, minced
1/2 cup *Whiplash Sauce*
  (or substitute D)
1 teaspoon dried basil
2 tablespoons unsalted butter
2 quarts chicken broth
14 small zucchini, scrubbed and chopped
  (about 8 cups)
3 tablespoons raw rice
1/3 cup cream cheese

In a large pot, combine the onions, garlic, Whiplash Sauce, basil, and butter and cook over moderate heat, stirring until the onion softens. Add the broth and zucchini, and bring the mixture to a boil. Stir in the rice. Cover the mixture, and simmer it, stirring occasionally, for 30 minutes or until the rice is tender. Stir the cream cheese into the hot mixture. Allow the soup to cool slightly.

In a blender or food processor, purée the soup in batches, transferring it as it is puréed to a tureen to serve warm. Or, if you prefer, reheat it briefly before serving.

Serves 4 to 6

Hot and Sour Soup

Lee Kum Kee's Hot and Sour Soup recipe is one of the fastest and simplest we've ever tasted. It takes only a few seconds to shred the ingredients, and this soup can stand on its own for a light dinner or lunch.

2 teaspoons *Lee Kum Kee Chicken Marinade*
  (or substitute soy sauce)
1/2 teaspoon cornstarch
2/3 cup cooked chicken or pork, shredded
1 cup chicken broth
1/2 package bean curd, cubed
2 dried black mushrooms, soaked
  and shredded
1 green onion, sliced
2 tablespoons shredded bamboo shoots
  (optional)
1 teaspoon *Panda Brand Sambal Oelek*
  ***Chili Sauce* (or substitute L)**
1 1/2 tablespoons white vinegar
1 egg, beaten

Combine the chicken marinade and cornstarch, and put the chicken or pork in the mixture to marinate briefly. Bring the chicken broth to a boil in a saucepan, and add the chicken and the remaining ingredients except the egg. Simmer over a low heat for approximately 2 minutes. Then stir in the beaten egg and serve immediately.

Serves 2

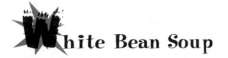hite Bean Soup

This quick and flavorful soup from Santa Fe Seasons can be made in about eight minutes. Talk about a good, fast meal for people on the go! The pesto and cheese add a little richness. Serve with some hot garlic toasts.

1 tablespoon olive oil
4 green onions, sliced
1 large garlic clove, minced
1 long, slender carrot, cut into thin rounds
1/4 cup dried beef, thinly sliced
2 cups cooked cannellini beans
2 cups water
1/3 cup *Santa Fe Seasons Pesto Santa Fe*
  (or substitute **R**)
Grated Parmesan cheese
Cilantro leaves

Heat the oil in a 4-quart pot. Add the onions, garlic, and carrot, and sauté the vegetables for 2 minutes. Add the beef, beans, and water and simmer for 5 minutes.

Ladle the soup into serving bowls. Spoon 1 to 2 tablespoons pesto over the top of each serving. Sprinkle with the Parmesan cheese and cilantro, and serve.

Serves 2 to 4

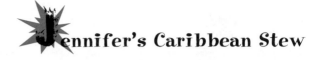ennifer's Caribbean Stew

The spicy peppers in Heat Wave Hot Sauce give this stew a special taste of St. Thomas, Virgin Islands, where it is manufactured. The stew is guaranteed to warm you up on a cold day, and it will even cool you down in heat-wave weather.

2 green bell peppers, chopped
3 celery stalks, chopped
6 garlic cloves, diced
2 medium onions, chopped
4 carrots, chopped
4 sprigs fresh thyme
5 fresh basil leaves, chopped
1/4 cup *Heat Wave Hot Sauce*
  (or substitute **G**)
1/4 teaspoon soy sauce
3/4 cup tomato sauce
2 1/2 cups water
1 to 2 pounds cubed beef, chicken, or pork
6 potatoes, cut into 1-inch cubes

Put the peppers, celery, garlic, onions, and carrots into a large pot. Add a little water and cook the vegetables, stirring, over medium heat. Add the thyme, basil, hot sauce, and soy sauce; continue to cook and stir the mixture until the onions are translucent. Add the tomato sauce, water, meat, and potatoes. Cover the pot, and simmer the stew for 1 hour. Serve the stew hot.

Serves 4 to 6

nappy Stew

Terri Deputy, the owner of Tuckie T's and the manufacturer of Hotsy Totsy products, created this spicy stew. It is simple to make, very nutritious, and excellent with jalapeño cornbread. Eat those chiles; they're good for you!

1 1/2 pound round steak, cut into
   bite-size pieces
1 large onion, chopped
1 tablespoon minced garlic
2 beef bouillon cubes
4 cups water
5 medium potatoes, peeled and cubed
3 medium carrots, cut into 1/2-inch rounds
3 celery stalks, chopped
1 medium zucchini, chopped
1 cup fresh corn kernels
1 cup green beans
3/4 cup peeled tomatoes
1 small can V-8 juice
1 1/2 cups hot *Hotsy Totsy Salsa*
   (or substitute **B**)
Salt, pepper, and seasoned salt to taste
Ground dried jalapeño chile to taste

In a large pot, simmer the beef, onion, garlic, and bouillon cubes in 2 cups of water for about 30 minutes. Add the remaining ingredients, and mix well. Add the remaining 2 cups water. Cover the pot, and simmer for 2 1/2 hours or until the vegetables are tender, adding more water if necessary. Serve the stew hot.

Serves 4

aco Soup

Despite the unlikely ingredients, Frank & Bryan Foods has created a delicious soup that carries a punch from the salsa. The soup can be prepared quickly, so, while it is cooking, whip up some cornbread to go with it.

1 pound lean ground beef
1 medium onion, chopped
3 cups corn kernels, cooked and drained
1 cup *Frank and Bryan's Sun Salsa*
   (or substitute **B**)
4 cups chopped peeled tomatoes
2 cups cooked pinto beans
1 package taco seasoning mix
1 package dried ranch dressing mix

In a large Dutch oven, brown the ground beef and onion. Drain off any excess fat. Add the remaining ingredients, and bring the soup to a boil. Reduce the heat, cover the pot, and simmer for approximately 1 hour. Serve the soup with corn tortillas or cornbread.

Serves 4 to 6

Mighty Meats

Rosemary and Red Serrano Roasted Pork Loin

This intensely flavored recipe is from Jay McCarthy, chef of Cascabel in San Antonio, who has been quite a hit at the Fiery Foods show with his dramatic demonstrations.

1/2 cup soy sauce
1/2 cup minced rosemary
6 to 8 red serrano chiles, seeded
1/3 cup minced garlic
1/4 cup cracked black peppercorns
1/3 cup peanut oil
4 pounds center-cut pork loin roast

Preheat the oven to 375 degrees.

In a blender, combine the soy sauce, rosemary, serranos, garlic, and black pepper. Blend, adding the oil slowly while the machine is running.

Rub the pork loin with the mixture, spreading it evenly. Roast the pork in the oven for 35 to 45 minutes.

Slice the pork, and serve it with new potatoes roasted with sage or potatoes mashed with horseradish.

Serves 6 to 8

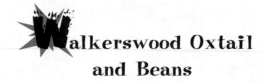

Walkerswood Oxtail and Beans

In Jamaica, oxtail is considered a special treat. This stewed oxtail from the Busha Browne Company, is thick and rich. If you have never tried oxtail stew, you should; it is extremely tasty and should be very thick.

3 pounds lean oxtail, jointed (or beef spareribs cut apart)
2 tablespoons vegetable oil
5 cups beef broth
4 Italian tomatoes
3 medium onions, chopped
1 garlic clove, finely minced
2 tablespoons *Busha Browne's Original Spicy Planters Sauce* (or substitute Worcestershire sauce)
2 teaspoons *Busha Browne's Pukka Hot Pepper Sauce* (or substitute D)
Salt and pepper to taste
2 cups broad beans (fava beans) or lima beans, cooked

Brown the prepared oxtail pieces in hot oil in a deep, heavy-bottomed saucepan. Add the beef broth, tomatoes, onions, garlic, and sauces. Cover the pan, and simmer until the oxtail is tender and the liquid has been reduced by one-half, about 2 hours.

Add salt and pepper and the beans, and cook until the beans are heated through. Serve hot.

Serves 6

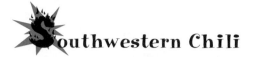

Southwestern Chili

This chili recipe comes from Laura Deck, owner of The Great Southwest Spice Company. A pot of chili cooking on the stove always gives off the most tempting aromas! Try this chili with hot cornbread and honey spiced with red chile powder.

1 pound ground beef (or, if you prefer a chunky chili, diced sirloin or tenderloin)

2 large yellow onions, diced

2 large bell peppers, diced

1/2 cup New Mexican green chiles, diced

2 tablespoons stemmed, seeded, and chopped jalapeño chiles

1/4 cup *Great Southwest All-Purpose Chili Seasoning* (or substitute O)

1 1/2 cups peeled and chopped tomatoes

1 to 2 cups water

In a large pot, brown the beef. Drain off any excess fat. Add the onions, bell peppers, green chiles, and jalapeños and cook, stirring, for 5 minutes. Add the seasoning and cook for an additional 5 minutes.

Add the stewed tomatoes, and bring the mixture to a boil. Add the water, return the mixture to a boil, and then reduce the heat. Cover the pot, and simmer at least 1 1/2 hours, stirring occasionally. Longer, slower cooking adds richness to the flavor.

Serve the chili hot.

Serves 2 to 4

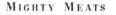

Santa Fe Beef Stroganoff

Sundance Foods gives a Southwestern taste twist on a continental classic. The seasoning mix, wine, and sour cream blend together to create a fine dish.

2 pounds boneless chuck roast, outer
fat removed, cut into 1/2- by 1/4- by
2-inch strips
3 tablespoons *Sundance Southwest*
Seasoning (or substitute A)
1 tablespoon olive oil
1 medium onion, chopped
5 tablespoons all-purpose flour
1 cup beef broth
1/3 cup sauterne or dry white wine
2 cups mushrooms, sliced
1/3 cup light sour cream or nonfat yogurt
Salt to taste
Cooked noodles, rice, or hot flour tortillas

Dust the meat with 1 tablespoon of the seasoning. Heat the olive oil in a Dutch oven. When the oil is hot, add the meat. Brown it quickly, tossing it to brown it evenly. Reduce the heat, push the meat to one side, and add the onion. Sauté the onion until it is transparent. Push the onion aside, and add the flour and remaining seasoning. Blend these into the drippings. Stir in the beef broth and wine. Cover the mixture, and cook until the beef is tender, about 1 hour.

Fifteen minutes before serving, fold in the mushrooms. Simmer for about 10 minutes, then fold in the sour cream. Heat the mixture briefly; do not allow it to boil. Season with salt.

Serve the stroganoff over noodles, rice or hot flour tortillas.

Serves 4

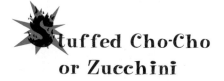

Stuffed Cho-Cho or Zucchini

In the United States, cho-cho is known as chayote, a squash that is available in some supermarkets and in Latin American markets. Its flavor is similar to that of zucchini. This recipe from Busha Browne is another taste treat from Jamaica. Cooked rice or pasta, if you have some left over, can be added to the meat mixture. Bell peppers and eggplants are also excellent for stuffing.

2 cho-chos or zucchini
1/2 pound ground beef or lamb
I onion, chopped
I teaspoon *Busha Browne's Original Spicy Planters Sauce* (or substitute Worcestershire sauce)
I tablespoon *Busha Browne's Spicy Tomato Love-Apple Sauce* (or substitute B)
Salt and pepper to taste
1/2 cup dried bread crumbs
I tablespoon grated and dried cheese (preferably cheddar)
4 teaspoons butter

Preheat the oven to 350 degrees.

Cut the cho-chos or zucchini in half lengthwise, and steam them until they are tender but not overdone. While the squash is cooking, sauté the ground meat in a heavy pan with the onion, sauces, and salt and pepper. When the squash is done, carefully scoop out the flesh, leaving about 1/4 inch on the skin, to form four shells. Add the cooked pulp to the meat mixture, and season to taste. Pack this mixture lightly into the squash shells.

Mix the bread crumbs with the cheese, and sprinkle this mixture over the stuffed squash. Place a pat of butter on each serving.

Bake the stuffed squash until it is golden brown on top and heated through, about 20 to 30 minutes. Serve it hot.

Serves 4

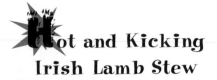

Hot and Kicking Irish Lamb Stew

From the National Hot Pepper Association comes this hot and spicy lamb stew, with flavors that sizzle! Betty Payton sure doesn't skimp on the chiles, and they blend well with the lamb and the vegetables.

1 1/2 pounds lamb, cut into 2-inch cubes
2 tablespoons vegetable oil
9 cups beef broth
2 cups water
3 medium potatoes, peeled and cut into 1-inch cubes
2 medium onions, chopped
2 celery stalks, sliced crosswise
2 carrots, sliced into rounds
5 jalapeño chiles, stemmed, seeded, and minced
3 yellow wax chiles, stemmed, seeded, and minced
3 small white turnips, peeled and cubed
1/4 teaspoon ground white pepper
1/4 teaspoon celery seed
1/4 teaspoon crushed dried marjoram leaves
1/8 teaspoon crushed dried thyme leaves

In a large skillet, brown the meat in the oil. Transfer the browned meat and the remaining ingredients into a crock pot, cover the pot, and cook on low heat for 8 to 10 hours, or until the meat and potatoes are done. Or, cook the stew on top of the stove at a higher temperature and with a shorter cooking time, approximately 2 hours, covered.

Serves 6 to 8

Texas Tasso

From Jay McCarthy, chef at Cascabel in San Antonio, comes this unique version of the traditional Cajun specialty. It can be shredded or ground before it is cooked—usually for breakfast.

1 9- to 12-pound leg of venison or boar, deboned, trimmed, and cut into 3-inch cubes.

Dry Ingredients:

1 cup paprika

1 cup ground dried cascabel or ancho chiles

1/2 cup ground black pepper

3 tablespoons ground dried habanero chiles, or 1/2 cup cayenne

1/2 cup red chile flakes

2 teaspoons dried sage

2 teaspoons dried marjoram

1/2 cup granulated garlic

Brine:

1 gallon water

2 cups salt, kosher or coarse pickling

1 cup sugar

1 cup crushed chiles de arbol or dried red pepper flakes

1 cup coarsely chopped fresh ginger

Combine the brine ingredients. In a covered crock or bowl, soak the meat in the brine for 2 to 4 days. Check the meat after 2 days by cutting a piece in half; the meat should be the same color all the way through.

Combine the dry ingredients. Remove the meat from the brine, and roll it in the chile mixture. Allow to dry in the refrigerator overnight.

Cold-smoke the meat over pecan wood for 4 to 6 hours.

After the meat has cooled, you can freeze it or keep it for a few days in the refrigerator. Grill or fry the meat as you would breakfast sausage or bacon.

Serves 10 to 12

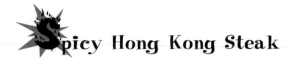 picy Hong Kong Steak

From Lee Kum Kee, a fine Chinese food company in Hong Kong and California, comes a unique recipe to liven up the palates of even the most jaded steak eaters. Many of us are used to grilled or broiled steaks, but these pan-fried steaks are truly a delicious change.

2 8-ounce sirloin steaks

1 tablespoon *Lee Kum Kee Oyster Sauce*
(or substitute other oyster sauce)

1 teaspoon *Lee Kum Kee Minced Garlic*
(or substitute fresh garlic)

1 teaspoon ground black pepper

3 tablespoons vegetable oil

1 tablespoon chopped onion

1 tomato, diced

1 tablespoon chopped celery

2 tablespoons American chili sauce

2 tablespoons ketchup

1 1/2 tablespoons sugar

6 tablespoons water

1 tablespoon minced parsley

Tenderize the steaks by pounding them lightly. Mix together the oyster sauce, garlic, and black pepper. Pour this mixture over the steaks, and marinate the steaks for 30 minutes.

Into a hot skillet, pour the 2 tablespoons of oil. Pan-fry the steaks until they are lightly browned on both sides. Remove the steaks to a warm platter.

Reheat the pan, and add 1 tablespoon oil. Stir-fry the onion, tomato, and celery together. Mix the chili sauce, ketchup, sugar, and water in a bowl, add the mixture to the stir-fry and mix well. Pour the sauce over the steaks, garnish with the parsley, and serve.

Serves 2

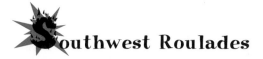outhwest Roulades

Scot Robinson of the Santa Fe Cookie Company says the stuffing can also be used in pounded, boneless chicken breasts. The following roulade, similar to the Argentine matambre, stuffed flank steak, is spicy and filling.

2 1/2 pounds round steak
1 1/2 cups *Santa Fe Cookie Company*
   Green Chile Pretzel Stuffing
   (see recipe on page 69)
6 1/4-inch-thick tomato slices
1/4 to 1/2 cup diced New Mexico
   green chiles
1 cup black or green olives, sliced
2 bacon slices
1 to 2 cups of dry red wine or beef broth

Preheat the oven to 325 degrees.

Pound the round steak until it is 1/4 to 3/8 inch thick. Try to keep the steak in the shape of a rectangle.

Spread the entire steak with the prepared stuffing. About 1 1/2 inches in from each end of the steak, place the tomato slices. Scatter the green chiles and the olives over the entire steak. Roll the steak up very tightly, and tie it in several places with string.

Place the rolled and tied steak in a small roasting pan or a heavy Dutch oven, cover with the two bacon slices, and add the wine or broth to the pan. Cover the pan.

Braise the steak in the oven for 2 to 2 1/2 hours, checking periodically to make sure there is liquid in the pan.

Remove the steak from the pan, and allow it to sit for a few minutes before slicing. Remove the string and slice the roulade into 1-inch pieces. Pour some of the pan juices over the top of the meat, if you like, and serve.

Serves 4 to 5

Hotsy Totsy Texas Tornadoes

These chile bombers are a real treat. Terri Deputy, the owner of Tuckie T's and the creator of Hotsy Totsy Products, says, "The company name comes from my grandmother, Tot Tuckness. And she was certainly a little hotsy-totsy in everyone's eyes."

3 to 4 pounds ground round beef
1 medium onion, chopped
1/2 teaspoon garlic powder
Ground black pepper to taste
1 pound longhorn cheese, grated
1 6-ounce can tomato sauce
1 12-ounce jar *Hotsy Totsy Salsa*
  (or substitute B)
2 dozen hard rolls, halved

Preheat the oven to 350 degrees.

In a large skillet, brown the ground beef and onion together. Remove the pan from the heat, and drain off the excess fat. Season the meat with the garlic powder and black pepper. Stir in the cheese, tomato sauce, and salsa.

Pinch the bread out of the center of the rolls, and fill the shells with the beef mixture. Put the two halves of each roll together again, wrap each roll in foil, and bake the rolls for 30 minutes. Serve them hot.

Serves 6 to 8

Gray's Spicy Prime Rib Roast

Excelsior Trading Company is the distributor for Gray's fine line of Jamaican products. Try this recipe from Gray's with your next rib roast, and surprise your family and friends with a tangy island-style roast.

1 3-pound rib roast
1/2 teaspoon dried thyme
1/2 teaspoon dried basil
1/2 teaspoon dried marjoram
1/2 teaspoon ground black pepper
3 tablespoons *Gray's Spicy Sauce*
  (or substitute G)
2 tablespoons teriyaki sauce
1 teaspoon sugar
5 garlic cloves, minced
6 green onions, finely sliced
3 Italian tomatoes

Wash the roast, and pat it dry. Mix all the ingredients together. With a sharp knife, make deep pockets in the roast, and insert the mixed ingredients. Marinate the roast in the refrigerator for 4 to 8 hours.

Preheat the oven to 400 degrees. Cook the roast for 1 hour, then reduce the temperature to 350 degrees and cook the roast until it is done to your taste. While the roast cooks, baste it occasionally with the pan juices.

Remove the roast from the oven. Slice it, and serve it with the pan juices on the side.

Serves 6

aco Pie

From Old El Paso Foods comes a great recipe for those of you on the go. Using El Paso's prepared products, you can present your family a tasty main dish in very little time.

1 pound ground beef
1 envelope (1 1/4 ounces) *Old El Paso Taco Seasoning Mix* **(or substitute A)**
1 cup *Old El Paso Thick 'n' Chunky Picante Sauce* **(or substitute B)**
1 egg
1 frozen *Pet-Ritz* **deep dish pie crust (or substitute any prepared pie crust)**
1 1/2 cups shredded jack cheese
1 4-ounce can *Old El Paso Chopped Green Chiles* **(or substitute fresh)**
1/3 cup broken *Old El Paso Tortilla Chips* **(or other brand)**

Place a baking sheet in the oven, and preheat the oven to 350 degrees.

In a large skillet, brown the ground beef. Drain off the excess fat. Add the taco seasoning mix and the picante sauce. Cook over a low heat for 5 to 8 minutes, and then remove the mixture from the heat. Stir in the egg, and set the pan aside.

Sprinkle the frozen pie crust with 1/2 cup cheese, and top the cheese with the green chiles. Pour the ground beef mixture evenly over the chiles, and top with the remaining 1 cup cheese. Sprinkle the tortilla chips over the top. Bake the pie for 20 to 25 minutes. Remove the pie from the oven. If you like, garnish the baked pie with shredded lettuce, olive slices, and additional picante before serving.

Serves 6

Lamb Chops with Minted Horseradish Sauce

From G. L. Mezzetta we have this recipe for a great horseradish topping for lamb chops. The judicious amount of horseradish is just enough to tickle the taste buds and give an added flavor to the lamb.

1 teaspoon butter or margarine
1 teaspoon chopped shallot
1/4 cup dry vermouth
1/4 cup chicken broth
2 tablespoons sour cream
1 tablespoon chopped fresh mint
1 tablespoon all-purpose flour
1 teaspoon *Tulelake Old Fashioned Horseradish* (or substitute freshly ground horseradish)
2 lamb loin chops

Preheat the broiler.

In a heavy saucepan, melt the margarine. Add the shallot, and sauté it over medium-high heat, stirring frequently, until the shallot is softened, about 1 1/2 minutes. Reduce the heat to low, and add the vermouth and the broth. Cook, stirring occasionally, for 4 to 5 minutes, until the liquid is reduced by half.

In a small bowl, mix the sour cream, mint, flour, and horseradish well. Stir this mixture into the vermouth mixture. Simmer the vermouth mixture, stirring frequently, until it is thickened; do not let the mixture boil. Set the pan aside, and keep the sauce warm.

Broil the lamb chops to taste, and top them with the sauce. Serve them at once.

Serves 2

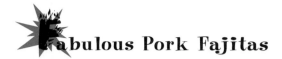

Fabulous Pork Fajitas

From Spirit Mesa in Tijeras, New Mexico, we offer this delicious fajitas recipe. The Southwest collides with the Caribbean in the combination of spices and orange juice here.

1 pound lean boneless pork
1 garlic clove, minced
1 teaspoon dried oregano, crumbled
1 teaspoon ground cumin
1 teaspoon seasoning salt
2 tablespoons orange juice
2 tablespoons *Spirit Mesa Oregano Vinegar*
   (or substitute C)
1 tablespoon vegetable oil
1 medium onion, sliced
1 green pepper, sliced
4 flour tortillas
Sliced green onion, shredded lettuce,
   and salsa, for garnish (optional)

Slice the pork across the grain into 1/8-inch strips.

Mix together the garlic, oregano, cumin, salt, orange juice, and vinegar. Marinate the pork strips in the mixture for 1 hour.

Heat the oil in a heavy skillet. Stir-fry the pork strips, onion, and bell pepper until the pork is no longer pink, about 3 to 5 minutes.

Serve the meat with the flour tortillas. Accompany the fajitas, if you like, with sliced green onion, shredded lettuce, and salsa.

Serves 4

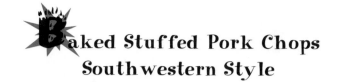

Baked Stuffed Pork Chops Southwestern Style

Debbie Wilmot of Gourmet Creations, Albuquerque, says these are the best pork chops you'll ever eat. The slight zing of the red chile jelly permeates the meat during the baking.

4 to 6 pork chops, 3/4- to 1-inch thick
1 cup dry bread crumbs
1/4 cup chopped celery
1/4 cup chopped onion
2 tablespoons minced parsley
1/4 teaspoon salt
1/8 teaspoon paprika
Milk or stock, to moisten the dressing
Gourmet Creations Red Chili Jelly
   (or substitute K)

Preheat the oven to 350 degrees. Cut a large pocket into the side of each chop.

In a bowl, mix together the vegetables, salt, and paprika. Fill the pockets with the dressing, and skewer the pockets shut.

Sear the chops on both sides in a hot skillet, and place them in a baking dish with a little milk or stock. Cover the dish and bake about 1 hour.

Spread a light glaze of chile jelly on each chop, and continue baking for 15 minutes, until the jelly melts into the chops.

Serves 4 to 6

Pork with Chocolate Mint Sauce

Spirit Mesa offers another mouthwatering recipe here. We just want to stop everything and cook this dish—now! It has elements of the famous mole *sauces of Mexico, which we think may have inspired this recipe.*

1 3-pound boneless pork loin
   roast, trimmed
3 tablespoons olive or other vegetable oil
1/3 cup water
1 large carrot, chopped
1 celery stalk, chopped
1 medium onion, chopped
1/2 cup blanched almonds
2 to 3 tablespoons chopped mint
2 garlic cloves, minced
1 1/2 ounces unsweetened chocolate
3 to 4 tablespoons *Spirit Mesa Mint Vinegar*,
   to taste (or substitute C)
1/2 teaspoon cayenne powder
3 tablespoons sugar
1 tablespoon raisins
1/4 cup pine nuts or slivered almonds

Preheat the oven to 350 degrees.

Heat 1 tablespoon of the oil in a large skillet, and add the roast. Brown the roast, turning it to sear all sides. Remove the roast from the heat, and place it in a 7- by 11-inch baking pan. Add the 1/3 cup water to the frying pan, stirring to release the browned bits, and pour this mixture over the roast.

In the same pan, heat the remaining 2 tablespoons of oil and sauté the carrot, celery, and onion over medium heat until the vegetables are soft. Add them to the pan containing the pork. Cover the pork and vegetables, and bake them for about 1 hour, or until the meat is no longer pink when cut.

While the meat is cooking, use blender or food processor to finely grind the blanched almonds, mint, and garlic together.

When the pork is done, remove the roast from the pan, and keep it warm.

Strain the pan juices and vegetables. Add water to the juices to make 1 cup, or boil them, uncovered, to reduce them to 1 cup. Pour the pan juices into the frying pan used to brown the meat, and set the pan over low heat. Add the chocolate, and stir until it is melted. Add the mint mixture, vinegar, cayenne, sugar, raisins, and pine nuts or slivered almonds; stir until the sauce thickens and has the texture of heavy cream.

Thinly slice the pork, and serve it. Offer the sauce to spoon over individual servings.

Serves 6 to 8

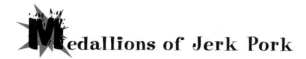edallions of Jerk Pork

Chip Hearn, the owner of Peppers in Dewey Beach, Delaware, really knows his way around the kitchen. He is also the owner of the Starboard Restaurant, which specializes in hot and spicy foods. Stop in and check out his collection of more than 1,800 hot sauces.

1 pork tenderloin (about 2 pounds)
1 teaspoon ground allspice
1 teaspoon brown sugar
1 teaspoon salt
1 teaspoon ground black pepper
1 tablespoon *Hot Bitch at the Beach* hot sauce (or substitute D)
4 garlic cloves, minced
2 teaspoons cider vinegar
1 medium onion, minced
1/2 teaspoon ground cinnamon
1/2 teaspoon ground nutmeg
10 green onions, chopped fine

Cut the tenderloin into 1/2- to 3/4-inch slices. Combine the remaining ingredients for the marinade. Marinate the meat in a covered container in the refrigerator for 3 hours.

Grill or pan-fry the pork about 3 minutes on each side. Serve it hot.

Serves 4 to 6

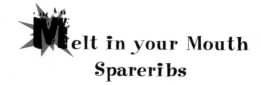elt in your Mouth Spareribs

Carol Norman and Nina Estes of Norman Bishop Mustards gave us this recipe, which uses one of their products. They recommend boiling the ribs to remove the excess fat and reduce the grilling time, so they won't be charred on the grill.

4 to 5 pounds pork spareribs
2 teaspoons salt
1 cup water
1 teaspoon celery seed
3 tablespoons *Norman Bishop Smokey Sweet Mustard* (or substitute H)
1/4 teaspoon *Tabasco Pepper Sauce* (or substitute D)
1/4 cup ketchup
1/2 teaspoon Worcestershire sauce
1/2 to 2 teaspoons red chile powder

Cut the ribs into serving-size pieces. Place the ribs in a large kettle or roaster. Sprinkle them with the 2 teaspoons salt. Cover the ribs with water, bring the water to a boil, and simmer the ribs for 1 hour.

Drain off the water and fat from the ribs. Combine the remaining ingredients for the basting sauce. Grill the ribs, brushing them occasionally with the sauce, for 10 to 15 minutes, turning frequently; or broil the ribs about 4 inches from the heat source in the oven, turning and basting often.

Serve the ribs hot.

Serves 5 to 6

Pork Loin in Adobo Sauce

This juicy, spicy recipe is from José Marmolejo, the owner of Don Alfonso Foods in Austin, Texas. We love to eat at José's house when we are in Austin because there is always something great cooking in the kitchen.

2 pounds boneless pork loin, trimmed
2 to 3 tablespoons vegetable oil
1/2 medium onion, chopped
1 garlic clove, minced
1 16-ounce jar *Don Alfonso's Adobo Sauce*
 (or substitute B)
Salt and pepper to taste

Cut the meat into 1-inch cubes, and brown it in the oil in a cast-iron skillet.

Add the remaining ingredients, cover the pan, and simmer the mixture on the stove for 30 minutes, adding water as needed to keep the meat covered with liquid.

Serve the pork and sauce hot with warm tortillas or rice.

Serves 4

San Antonio Grilled Chicken

We thank Kim Wall of Sundance Foods for this recipe. The combination of flavors gives the chicken some character.

2 large whole chicken breasts
 (about 3/4 pounds each) split,
 boned, and skinned
1 cup *Sundance Salsa* (or substitute B)
3 tablespoons dark brown sugar
4 teaspoons Dijon-style mustard
Salt to taste

Pound the breasts to a 1/2-inch thickness. Combine the Sundance Salsa, sugar, mustard, and salt, and mix well. Place the chicken on a grill over hot coals, or under a broiler, about 6 inches from the heat source. Brush the breasts generously with some of the salsa mixture. Grill or broil the chicken for 6 to 8 minutes, or until it is cooked through.

Heat the remaining sauce, and serve it with the chicken.

Serves 2

Boneless Chicken or Veal Scallops in Pineapple Habanero Mustard Sauce

Isla Vieques Condiment Company offers another way to add some spice and change to complement chicken. The tropical, Caribbean flavors are evident in the combo of peppers and fruit. Serve this recipe with rice pilaf.

2 tablespoons unsalted butter

3 tablespoons olive oil

3 green onions, chopped

1 1/2 pounds boned chicken breasts or veal scallops, pounded to 1/4-inch thickness

Salt and pepper to taste

1/3 cup dry white wine

1/3 cup *Isla Vieques Pineapple Habanero Mustard* (or substitute H)

1/2 cup heavy cream

Melt the butter and oil together in a large skillet. Add the green onions, and sauté them over low heat for 5 minutes; do not let them brown.

Raise the heat, add the meat, and season it with salt and pepper. Cook veal scallops 1 minute per side; chicken breasts 3 to 4 minutes per side.

Remove the meat from the skillet, and keep it warm. Add the wine to the skillet and bring it to a boil. Cook the wine until it is reduced to a few spoonfuls.

Whisk in the mustard and heavy cream, and boil the sauce for 2 minutes. Taste the sauce, and correct the seasoning.

Arrange the meat on a serving platter, spoon the sauce over the meat, and serve.

Serves 4 to 6

Hot and Sweet Mustard Chicken with Vegetable Stuffing

The Norman Bishop Mustard Company tells us this is the easiest, best-tasting chicken dish they have ever prepared. The unusual vegetable stuffing, paired with the citrus and the Norman Bishop Hot and Sweet Mustard, is indeed a taste treat.

1 large onion, thinly sliced
2 cups shredded zucchini
1/2 cup shredded carrots
2 garlic cloves, crushed
3 tablespoons butter or margarine
1 1/2 teaspoons dried tarragon
2 tablespoons plus 2 teaspoons lemon juice
1/2 teaspoon grated lemon peel
1/4 cup *Norman Bishop Hot and Sweet*
  ***Mustard* (or substitute H)**
Salt and pepper to taste
1 whole fryer chicken

In a skillet, sauté the onion, zucchini, carrots, and one crushed garlic clove in 1 tablespoon butter or margarine until the vegetables are soft but not browned. Stir in 1/2 teaspoon tarragon, 2 teaspoons lemon juice, the lemon peel, and the mustard. Add the salt and pepper, and let the mixture cool.

Preheat the oven to 375 degrees, or prepare a grill for outdoor roasting. Stuff the chicken with vegetable mixture.

In a small pan, melt the remaining 2 tablespoons butter or margarine. Add one crushed garlic clove, 1 teaspoon tarragon, and 2 tablespoons lemon juice.

Roast the chicken in the oven for 1 1/4 to 1 1/2 hours, basting frequently with the butter or margarine mixture, and covering the chicken loosely with foil if the skin browns too quickly.

Or roast the chicken in a covered grill about 1 1/2 hours, checking occasionally to make sure that the chicken isn't burning.

Serve the chicken hot.

Serves 4

Roasted Chicken with Green Chile Pretzel Stuffing

This unusual recipe makes a great stuffing for chicken, game hens, or even turkey. Imagine the family's surprise at Thanksgiving! The Santa Fe Cookie Company's pretzels are also great with beer during those fall football games.

I 4- to 5-pound chicken
2 1/2 cups *Santa Fe Cookie Company Green Chile Pretzels*, **coarsely crushed (or substitute crushed pretzels with I teaspoon red chile powder)**
3 to 5 tablespoons butter
I cup sliced mushrooms
I cup diced onion
2 garlic cloves, minced
1/2 cup pine nuts
1/2 cup chicken broth
Additional melted butter or olive oil, for basting the chicken

Preheat the oven to 325 degrees. Rinse and pat dry the chicken.

Put the coarsely crushed pretzels into a large bowl. Melt 3 tablespoons butter in a medium skillet. Add the sliced mushrooms, and briefly sauté them. Remove them to the bowl with the pretzels.

Return the skillet to the heat, and add a tablespoon or two more butter, if necessary. When the butter is sizzling, add the onion, and sauté it for a minute. Add the garlic, and sauté for 30 seconds more, taking care not to burn the garlic. Add the onion and garlic to the pretzels and mushrooms.

Add the pine nuts to the bowl, and toss lightly. Add the chicken broth, a little at a time, until the mixture is well moistened but not soupy. Loosely stuff the mixture into the chicken cavity; it needs a little room to expand. Close the cavity by pulling the skin across in opposite directions and securing the skin with a toothpick or two. Place the chicken in a roasting pan and coat it with olive oil or butter. Roast the chicken for 1 1/2 to 2 hours, until it is fully cooked but not dry. If it starts to get too brown, cover it with a tent of aluminum foil.

Serve the chicken hot.

Serves 6 to 8

Zack's Chicken and Andouille Sausage Gumbo

Jim Akers and John Hurt of Zack's Foods shared this terrific gumbo recipe, which calls for their Zack's Virgin Habanero Sauce. Andouille sausage can be found at many specialty food markets.

4 large whole chicken breasts
4 quarts water, seasoned with salt and
  ground red chile
6 garlic cloves, chopped
1 large white onion, chopped
1 bell pepper, chopped
1 pound andouille sausage, chopped
1 14 1/2-ounce can tomatoes, chopped
2 bay leaves
1 teaspoon poultry seasoning
1 diced hot red chile, crushed
4 dashes Worcestershire sauce
1 tablespoon black or assorted
  whole peppercorns
1/2 teaspoon ground nutmeg
1/2 cup white wine
1/2 teaspoon dried thyme
1 1/2 tablespoon curry powder
1 package frozen okra
1 tablespoon minced parsley
1 tablespoon filé gumbo
1/2 teaspoon *Zack's Virgin Habanero Sauce*
  (or substitute **G**)
4 to 5 slices bacon, cut into small pieces
1 cup all-purpose flour

1 cup vegetable oil
1 package Sazon Goya con Culontro y
  Achiote (optional—available in Latin
  markets)

Boil the chicken breasts in the seasoned water for 20 minutes, until they are tender. Remove the chicken from the water, and cool. Debone the chicken, chop it, and set it aside. Add all of the other ingredients to the liquid except the flour, oil, and *Sazon*, and boil the gumbo over medium heat for 2 or more hours.

While the gumbo cooks, combine the flour and the oil in a small, heavy saucepan. Bring the mixture to a boil, and let it boil moderately, as you stir constantly, until the roux turns a milk chocolate-brown color (this takes 30 to 40 minutes). Remove the pan from the heat, and continue stirring for 4 to 5 minutes as the roux continues to cook. Let the roux stand for 30 minutes or so and then drain off the excess oil. (The roux can be made ahead and kept in the refrigerator.)

Add the roux to the gumbo, a little at a time, until it is dissolved in the liquid.

Add the chicken, and, if you like, the *Sazon*. Simmer the gumbo for 30 to 45 minutes more.

Serve the gumbo over white rice with crusty french bread.

Serves 6 to 8

Chicken Fajitas

We would like to thank Hunter-McKenzie and the McIlhenny Company for this refreshing, hot and spicy recipe. The spicy chicken is somewhat tamed by the salsa, corn relish, and accompaniments.

4 boned and skinned chicken breast halves

2 teaspoons ground cumin

1 1/2 teaspoons *Tabasco Pepper Sauce* (or substitute D)

1 teaspoon chile powder

1/2 teaspoon salt

Spicy Tomato Salsa:

1 large ripe tomato, diced

1 tablespoon chopped cilantro

1 tablespoon lime juice

1 teaspoon *Tabasco Pepper Sauce* (or substitute D)

1/4 teaspoon salt

Corn Relish:

1 1/2 cups cooked and drained corn kernels

1/2 cup diced green bell pepper

1 tablespoon lime juice

1/2 teaspoon *Tabasco Pepper Sauce* (or substitute D)

1/4 teaspoon salt

8 flour tortillas

1 tablespoon vegetable oil

3 large green onions, cut into 2-inch pieces

1/2 cup shredded cheddar cheese

Sliced avocado and sour cream, as accompaniments

Preheat the oven to 350 degrees.

Cut the chicken breasts into 1/2-inch strips. In a large bowl, toss the chicken strips with the cumin, Tabasco sauce, chile powder, and salt. Set the seasoned chicken aside.

Combine the spicy tomato salsa ingredients in a separate bowl. In another bowl, combine the corn relish ingredients.

Wrap the tortillas in foil; heat them in the oven for 10 minutes or until they are warm.

While the tortillas are warming, heat the vegetable oil over medium-high heat in a large skillet. Add the chicken mixture, and cook it for 4 minutes, stirring frequently. Add the green onions, and cook 1 minute longer, or until the chicken is browned and tender.

To serve the fajitas, set out the warmed tortillas along with the chicken, salsa, corn relish, cheddar cheese, avocado, and sour cream.

To assemble the fajitas, place the strips of chicken in the center of each tortilla, and add salsa, corn relish, and some of each accompaniment. Fold over the bottom quarter and both sides of the tortilla to cover the filling, and enjoy.

Serves 4

Avocado Chicken Tostadas

We *thank one of our longest exhibitors and support- ers, Bueno Foods of Albuquerque, for contributing this recipe for crispy, spicy tostadas.*

1 teaspoon olive oil

2 teaspoons lemon juice

1 bay leaf, cut into 4 pieces

1/2 teaspoon dried parsley flakes

1 teaspoon salt

1/8 teaspoon *Bueno Granulated Garlic*
   (or substitute fresh)

3 boned and skinned chicken breasts,
   cut into cubes

2 avocados

1/4 cup *Bueno Frozen Green Chile*
   (or substitute fresh New Mexican)

2 teaspoons chopped green onions

1/4 cup minced onion

4 *Bueno Tostada Shells*

1 large tomato, chopped

1 cup shredded jack cheese

In a saucepan over medium heat, heat the oil, 1 teaspoon lemon juice, the bay leaf, the parsley flakes, 1/2 teaspoon salt, and the garlic.

Add the chicken. Cook, stirring occasionally, until it is cooked through. Remove the saucepan from the heat.

In a bowl, mash the avocados with 1 teaspoon lemon juice and 1/2 teaspoon salt. Add the green chile, green onions, and onion. Stir until they are blended.

Spread the avocado mixture onto the tostada shells, and arrange the cooked chicken on top.

Garnish with the chopped tomato and shredded cheese, and enjoy.

Serves 4 to 8

picy Chicken Stir Fry

Gourmet Creations offers this recipe for a quick and tasty stir-fry. We think it sounds like a great year-round dish, but it especially appeals to us as a summer one, with the addition of fresh vegetables right out of the garden—squash, snow peas, or sliced baby carrots.

1 pound boned chicken breast, cut into
** 1/2-inch cubes**
1/3 cup *Gourmet Creations Flaming Chile Oil*
** (or substitute S)**
1 pound broccoli florets, cut into
** bite-size pieces**
8 ounces fresh mushrooms, sliced
1 cup chicken broth
1/8 cup chopped cashews
Cooked rice

In a large skillet or wok, heat the *Flaming Chili Oil*. Add the chicken, cook it, stirring constantly, until the meat turns white on all sides.

Add the broccoli, mushrooms, and broth (you may add or substitute other ingredients), and cover the pan. Cook for 4 minutes more. Sprinkle with the cashews just before serving.

Serve the stir-fry immediately over hot rice.

Serves 3 to 4

amaican Jerk-Roasted Chicken

Winston Stona of the Busha Browne Company gave us this recipe. The term jerk has nothing to do with one's personality; it refers to a Jamaican specialty that originated with the Maroons, who seasoned their meat and smoked it to preserve it, to fortify themselves as they hid out in the cockpit country of Jamaica to avoid capture and slavery. Serve this delicious historical dish with seasoned rice, fried plantains, a green salad, and fresh fruit.

1 4-pound roasting chicken
1 tablespoon lime or lemon juice
3 tablespoons *Busha Browne's Jerk Seasoning*
** (or substitute Q)**

Preheat the oven to 325 degrees.

Rub the whole chicken inside and out with the lime or lemon juice. Spread the jerk seasoning over the whole chicken, rub the seasoning in well, and allow the chicken to marinate in the refrigerator for at least 2 hours. Roast the chicken in the oven for 1 1/2 to 2 hours, basting continually with the pan drippings, until the chicken is done; do not overcook it. Carve the chicken on a platter, and accompany it with soothing fruit such as pineapple or mango.

Variations: Cut up the chicken and grill it. Prepare whole fish in the same way.

Serves 6

Rio Verde Chicken Enchiladas

Thank you to Goldwater's Foods of Arizona for this recipe. The dish is very rich and delicious. The tomatillos add a wonderful, unusual taste. For a lighter meal, you may want to reduce the number of eggs (or try using two eggs and something like Eggbeaters, and cut back a little on the cheese.) Enjoy the wonderful flavors either way.

2 whole chicken breasts, cooked
   and shredded
1 cup chopped onion
1 cup grated jack cheese
1/4 cup grated Parmesan cheese
1/4 cup vegetable oil
8 corn tortillas
2 cups heavy cream
1 jar Goldwater's *Rio Verde Tomatillo Sauce*
   (or substitute other tomatillo salsa or B)
4 eggs
2 cups grated cheddar cheese

Preheat the oven to 350 degrees.

In a bowl, combine the chicken, onion, and white cheeses. Heat the oil, and fry the tortillas just until they are soft. Drain them on paper towels.

Divide the chicken mixture in the tortillas. Roll the tortillas, and lay them seam side down in a medium baking dish.

Beat together the salsa, whipping cream, and eggs. Cover the tortillas with the sauce, and sprinkle them with cheddar cheese. Bake the enchiladas for 30 minutes.

Variations: For a festive touch, garnish with guacamole, sour cream, shredded lettuce, chopped tomatoes, or chopped black olives. Try substituting spinach for chicken, and create a vegetarian delight!

Serves 4

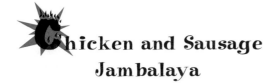

Chicken and Sausage Jambalaya

Scott Byron Landry, the owner and chef of Byron's Catering in Lake Charles, Louisiana, gave us this recipe for a mellow, tasty dish. The smells that emanate from the jambalaya as it cooks will let you know why this dish is one of the hallmarks of Creole cookery. You can adjust the heat level by adding more or less of the cayenne pepper.

1 pound smoked sausage
2 tablespoons margarine or butter
1 tablespoon all-purpose flour
3/4 cup diced onions
1/4 cup diced bell peppers
1/3 cup sliced celery
1/2 teaspoon garlic powder
1 cup tomato purée
2 cups chicken stock
2 teaspoons salt
1/2 teaspoon cayenne powder
1 tablespoon white sugar
1/8 teaspoon dried oregano
1/2 bay leaf, crushed
1 pound cooked chicken breasts
1 cup raw rice
1 tablespoon minced green onions

Cut the sausage into 1/2-inch pieces. Sauté the sausage in the butter or margarine in a Dutch oven until the sausage is light brown. Add the flour, and cook, stirring frequently, until the mixture is golden brown.

Add the onions, green peppers, celery, and garlic powder. Cook until the vegetables become soft.

Combine the tomato purée with the chicken broth and add them to the vegetable mixture. Add the salt, cayenne, sugar, oregano, and crushed bay leaves, and bring the mixture to a boil. Cut the chicken into pieces, 2 1/2 inches by 5 inches wide. Add the chicken to the vegetable mixture, and bring the mixture to a simmer.

Wash the raw rice three or four times by covering it with water, rubbing the rice between your hands, and pouring off the water, until the wash water is almost clear. Add the rice to the mixture, and cover the Dutch oven. Simmer the Jambalaya for approximately 20 minutes, folding the mixture frequently from side to middle and from top to bottom to keep the rice from sticking. Stir in the green onion. Cook approximately 5 minutes, or until the rice is tender and moist, not hard.

Serves 4 to 6

eanutty Chicken

Ken and Wendy Roda are the creators of Hot Heads hot sauce products, as well as distributors of hot sauces from around the world. The Mean Green sauce and the peanuts, served over chicken breasts, add interest and crunch to this dish.

All-purpose flour, to dredge the breasts
4 chicken breasts, boned, skinned, and split
Peanut oil or vegetable oil
I cup roasted and chopped peanuts
2 celery ribs, coarsely chopped
2 green onions, sliced
I to 2 tablespoons all-purpose flour
1/4 to I teaspoon *Hot Heads Mean Green Hot Sauce* (or substitute B)
I 1/2 cups chicken broth

Lightly flour the chicken breasts. Heat the oil in a skillet large enough to hold all the chicken. Place the chicken in the oil, and sear both sides. Turn down the heat, and add the peanuts, celery, and green onions. Sauté for I 1/2 minutes.

Stir in I to 2 tablespoons of flour to absorb the oil. Stir in the Mean Green, add the chicken broth, and simmer until the chicken is done. Place the breasts on a platter, and top them with the sauce. Serve over spinach fettucine and add a salad of tomatoes and cucumbers.

Serve the chicken hot.

Serves 4

Stimulating Seafood

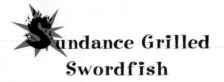

Sundance Grilled Swordfish

Kim Wall of Sundance Foods, in Milwaukee, spends as much time as she can in Florida with her parents, and this recipe is the result of one of her visits. Kim said if they don't catch enough fish for dinner, they save what they've caught for breakfast the next day, when they can have this dish. We could live like that; pass the Sundance Seasoning for the eggs and hash browns!

**2 tablespoons olive oil, plus more for
  brushing the grill**
1/4 cup lime juice
Sundance Southwest Seasoning
  (or substitute A)
**4 6-ounce swordfish (or tuna, marlin,
  amberjack, or mahi mahi fillets)**

In a small bowl, whisk the 2 tablespoons olive oil and lime juice together. Brush both sides of the fillets with the mixture. Brush a hot grill with olive oil.

Apply a heavy coat of Sundance Southwest Seasoning to each fillet, and grill the fillets for 3 to 5 minutes per side for every 1 inch of thickness. Do not overcook the fish, or it will be very tough.

While the fillets are grilling, shake on additional seasoning to taste.

Variation: To pan-fry the fish, heat a large skillet over medium heat. When the skillet is hot, add 1 tablespoon olive oil and the fillets. Fry them 3 to 4 minutes per side.

Serves 4

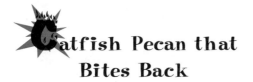

Catfish Pecan that Bites Back

The manufacturers of Ring of Fire Hot Sauce offer their tasty, crunchy recipe for catfish, featuring their sauce. Some people won't eat catfish because it can bear off-flavors, but the farmed catfish now widely sold is delicate and flaky.

1/4 cup dry bread crumbs
3/4 cup finely chopped pecans
6 6- to 8-ounce boned and skinned catfish
   fillets
1/4 cup *Ring of Fire Hot Sauce*
   (or substitute D)
1/4 cup butter or margarine

Put the bread crumbs and pecans into a food processor, and pulse until the pecans are finely ground. Coat the fillets with the hot sauce, then roll them in the pecan mixture.

Melt the butter or margarine in a frying pan. Fry the fish over medium heat until it is cooked through and the pecan crust is golden brown (approximately 3 minutes on each side).

Serve the fish, if you like, with wild rice and steamed asparagus with lemon juice. For a gourmet touch, present the fish on a bed of wilted spinach.

Serves 6

Cod Fish Fritters

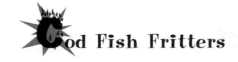

Rainforest Food Products imports the Bello products from Dominica, West Indies. We thank Rainforest for sharing this traditional Caribbean recipe, which is enlivened with Bello's fine hot pepper sauce.

2 cups all-purpose flour
1 teaspoon baking powder
3 eggs
4 cups milk
1 tablespoon *Bello Hot Pepper Sauce*
   (or substitute D or G)
1 teaspoon minced onion
1 teaspoon minced garlic
1 tablespoon minced celery
1 1/2 teaspoons minced chives
1 1/2 teaspoons dried thyme
2 pounds cod or other white fish
   fillets, flaked
Vegetable oil, for frying

In a bowl, combine the flour and baking powder. Beat in the eggs, one at a time, and then the milk and hot sauce. Stir in the remaining ingredients. Mold the mixture into 1-inch balls.

Heat the oil in a heavy pot. Spoon the codfish balls into the hot oil, and cook until they are a golden brown. Drain the fritters well, and serve with your favorite sauce.

Serves 8

Royal Seafood Court Bouillon Lerida

We thank Charley Addison for this great seafood recipe. Charley named his company after an old Cajun who befriended him as a child; some people referred to old Oscar as the Crazy Cajun, so Charley has kept Oscar's memory alive with Crazy Cajun Enterprises. Don't let the long list of ingredients stop you from making this bouillon; you probably have most of them on hand, and the finished product is delicious.

1/4 cup all purpose flour

1/2 cup vegetable oil

3/4 cup chopped onion

3/4 cup chopped green bell pepper

1 cup chopped celery

3 cloves minced garlic

1/2 teaspoon crushed hot red pepper

1 cup *Crazy Cajun Gumbo (no substitution)*

3/4 cup *Crazy Cajun All Purpose and Barbecue Sauce* (or substitute F)

1/2 teaspoon salt

3 bay leaves

2 cups chicken or clam broth

1/2 cup dry white wine

4 thin lemon slices

2 tablespoons chopped fresh parsley

2 pounds fresh fish, oysters, shrimp, or scallops, or a combination of these

In a 4-quart or 6-quart Dutch oven, stir together the flour and oil until the mixture is smooth. Cook it over medium-high heat for about 8 minutes, stirring constantly, to make a roux. Reduce the heat to medium and continue to cook, stirring for about 10 minutes more, until you have a reddish brown roux.

Add the onion, bell pepper, celery, and garlic, and cook for 15 minutes, stirring often. You may need to add about 1/4 cup more vegetable oil at this point.

Stir in the hot pepper, gumbo, barbecue sauce, salt, bay leaves, and broth. Bring the mixture to a simmer, and simmer it, uncovered, for about 30 minutes.

Stir in the wine, lemon, and parsley. Bring the mixture to a simmer again and add the seafood. Simmer for another 6 minutes. Turn off the heat, and let the bouillon stand, covered, for 20 minutes before serving.

Serve the soup over rice or pasta.

Serves 4

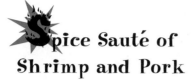

Spice Sauté of Shrimp and Pork

Chef Jim Heywood works for the CIA—the Culinary Institute of America in Hyde Park, New York. This recipe is an example of the imaginative hot and spicy dishes he makes during his demonstrations at the Fiery Foods Show.

20 to 25 medium shrimp, peeled, deveined, and cut into 2 pieces each
Salt and pepper to taste
1/2 pound boneless pork, cut into 1/2-inch cubes
2 tablespoons olive oil
1/3 cup minced shallots
3 minced garlic cloves
2 yellow bell peppers, chopped
4 jalapeño chiles, stemmed and seeded, and cut into strips
1 cup dried strawberries or cranberries
1/3 cup white wine
2 tablespoons balsamic vinegar
2 cups canned chicken gravy
1/2 cup tomato sauce
Cooked shell pasta
1 cup coarsely grated pepper jack cheese
1/2 cup minced cilantro

Sprinkle the shrimp with salt and pepper. Heat the olive oil in a skillet, and sauté the shrimp and pork until the pork is lightly browned, about 5 minutes. Remove the skillet from the heat and remove the shrimp and pork to a bowl. Keep the shrimp and pork warm in the oven.

Add to the skillet the shallots, garlic, bell pepper, and jalapeños, and sauté briefly, keeping the peppers crisp. Add the dried strawberries or cranberries, wine, and vinegar. Stir well, and bring the mixture to a boil. Add the chicken gravy and tomato sauce. Stir well, and bring the mixture to a boil again, adding some chicken stock if the mixture is too thick. Add the pork and shrimp, stir well, and cook for 2 minutes.

Serve the mixture over cooked shell pasta, garnished with the cheese and cilantro.

Serves 4 to 6

# Barbecued Salmon Fillets

This is a delicious and unusual way to serve salmon. Accompany it with a chilled pasta salad and enjoy the contrast in flavors. Flowers of the Flame products are made by Creative Chef Foods.

3/4 pound butter or margarine
2 garlic cloves, minced or crushed
1 1/2 tablespoons dry mustard
1 1/2 tablespoons soy sauce
1/3 cup dry sherry
Flower of the Flames Bar-Be-Que Sauce
  (or substitute F)
6 to 8 pounds salmon fillets

In a saucepan, combine the butter, garlic, mustard, soy sauce, sherry, and sauce. Stir the mixture over medium heat until the butter is melted. Brush about half the mixture lightly over the salmon. Grill the salmon on foil over a drip pan and over medium hot coals. Cover the grill and adjust the vents to maintain an even heat. Grill the salmon for 15 to 20 minutes.

Transfer the salmon from the foil to a serving platter. Cover the salmon with the remaining butter mixture, and serve at once.

Serves 10

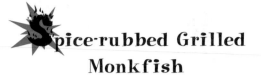# Spice-rubbed Grilled Monkfish

Monkfish is mild-flavored, slightly sweet, and textured, when cooked, like red meat. Ask your seafood supplier for a fish similar in texture if monkfish is not available. Our thanks to Joe Dulle of Rio Diablo Hot Sauce for the recipe. Joe was one of the hot-sauce winners in the Austin Chronicle's annual hot-sauce contest.

1/4 cup ground cumin
2 tablespoons paprika
2 tablespoons chile powder
1 tablespoon cracked black pepper
1 tablespoon brown sugar
2 tablespoons dried oregano
1 to 2 1/2 pounds monkfish fillets
***Rio Diablo Hot Sauce*, to taste**
  (or substitute D or G)

Combine the spices, sugar, and oregano in a bowl. Rub the fillets thoroughly with the mixture. Over a medium-hot fire, grill the fish on both sides for approximately 15 minutes total, until the outside of the fish becomes brown.

Serve the fish with the hot sauce on the side.

Serves 2 to 4

Grilled Swordfish with Adeline's Gourmet Kiwi Salsa

Adeline Reyes of Adeline's Gourmet Foods is the creator of three exotic salsas: mango, coconut, and kiwi. In this recipe, the combination of the kiwi salsa and the golden raisins complements the taste of the fish.

1/4 cup olive oil
4 6- to 8-ounce swordfish steaks
  (3/4-inch thick)
Flour, for dredging the fish
1 onion, minced
1/4 cup dry white wine
1 jar Adeline's Gourmet Kiwi Salsa
  (or substitute J)
1/3 cup golden raisins

Heat the oil in a large, heavy skillet over high heat.

Season the fish with salt and pepper. Coat the fish lightly with the flour, and lay the fish in the skillet. Cook the fish until it is golden brown, about 2 minutes per side, and transfer it to a plate.

Add the onion and white wine to the same skillet. Reduce the heat to medium, and cook for about 4 minutes.

Add to the skillet the kiwi salsa and the golden raisins. Cook this mixture for 2 minutes.

Return the fish to the skillet, and spoon the sautéed ingredients over the fish. Cook until the fish is cooked through, about 2 minutes. Transfer the fish to serving plates, and pour the sautéed ingredients over it.

Serves 4

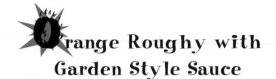range Roughy with Garden Style Sauce

This delicious dish from Bueno Foods is great for those of you on a low-fat or low-sodium diet. The spicy sauce satisfies the taste buds. You can substitute any firm, mild fish for the orange roughy.

1 tablespoon olive oil
1 small onion, chopped
1 small green bell pepper, chopped
1 13-ounce carton *Bueno Green Chile Sauce* (garden-style) (or substitute B)
1 pound orange roughy fillets

In a large skillet, heat the oil.

Sauté the onion and bell pepper until they are soft. Add the chile sauce, and bring the mixture to a simmer. Add the fillets to the sauce. Spoon the sauce over the fillets, and cover the pan. Reduce the heat, and simmer over low heat until the fish is cooked through, 15 to 20 minutes.

Serve the fish and sauce over steamed rice.

Serves 2

Caribbean Smoked Fish Pie

Richard Gardner of California-Antilles imports the West Indies Creole Sauce used in this recipe. The mixture of flavors in this pie is a real taste treat, and the smoked fish makes the pie an unusual entrée.

1 teaspoon lime juice
1/2 cup chopped onions
2 garlic cloves, minced
1 cup tomato purée
1 teaspoon *West Indies Creole Gourmet Hot Pepper Sauce* (or substitute G)
1 teaspoon salt
1 egg, beaten
1 cup smoked fish, flaked
1 9-inch unbaked pie shell
1/4 cup roasted almonds, chopped

Preheat the oven to 350 degrees.

In a bowl, combine the first 6 ingredients and mix well. Stir in the egg and the fish. Add the fish mixture to the pie shell, sprinkle roasted almonds on top, and bake for approximately 25 minutes.

Serve the pie with a fresh green salad.

Serves 6

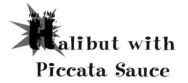Halibut with Piccata Sauce

Chef Eddie Adams offers this spicy piccata sauce for halibut. Make it at home, or order it at Eddie's restaurant, The Gulf Coast Eatery, in Albuquerque.

1/2 cup butter or margarine
1/4 cup brined capers, with
  1 tablespoon brine
Juice of 1 large lemon
1 garlic clove, minced
1/4 cup cold water
1/2 tablespoon cornstarch
1 teaspoon *Eddie's Cajun Flavors Seafood Spice* (or substitute **N**)
2 halibut fillets, baked or broiled

Melt the butter in a 2-quart saucepan. Add the capers, brine, and lemon juice, and bring the mixture to a boil.

In a small bowl, stir the water into the cornstarch. Add this mixture, the garlic, and the spices to the saucepan, and heat, stirring constantly, until the sauce thickens.

Serve the sauce hot over the halibut fillets.

Serves 2

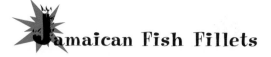Jamaican Fish Fillets

We thank Valerie and Lloyd Webster of Anjo's Imports for this very tropical-tasting dish, with a strong Jamaican influence in the spice combination.

1 pound white fish fillets
1/2 cup lemon juice
1 tablespoon *Island Treasure Spicy Sauce* (or substitute **G**)
1 heaping tablespoon dry jerk seasoning (or substitute **Q**)
1/2 teaspoon ground ginger
1/2 teaspoon ground allspice
1/2 medium onion, chopped
1 tablespoon vinegar
Chopped tomatoes and parsley, for garnish

Marinate the fish in the lemon juice for 5 minutes. Drain off the juice and wipe the fish dry.

In a small bowl, mix the remaining ingredients except the garnish. Rub the fish with the mixture, and marinate the fish for about 30 minutes.

Preheat the oven to 325 degrees.

Bake the fish until it is tender, about 20 minutes. Garnish it with tomatoes and parsley, and serve it hot.

Serves 2

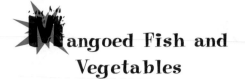

Mangoed Fish and Vegetables

This superb tropical dish from Isla Vieques of Puerto Rico features the unusual combination of bamboo shoots and mango preserves. A bonus to this dish is that it is fast and very easy to prepare.

1 cup bamboo shoots, sliced lengthwise
1 medium cucumber, seeded and chopped
1 cup button mushrooms, sliced
Salt and pepper to taste
4 teaspoons vegetable oil
1 pound fish fillets
3/4 cup flour
4 teaspoons soy sauce
2 tablespoons rice wine vinegar
  or white vinegar
1/2 cup fish stock
1/4 cup *Isla Vieques Jam 'n' Mango Preserves*
  (or substitute K)
1 tablespoon cornstarch

Season the vegetables with the salt and pepper. Heat the oil in a skillet, and sauté the vegetables for 2 minutes. Remove the skillet from the heat.

Oil and heat another skillet. Toss the fish in the flour, and fry the fish until it is golden brown.

In a small bowl, mix the soy sauce, vinegar, fish stock, mango preserves, and cornstarch together and add this mixture to the vegetables. Cook for 1 minute.

Pour the sauce over the fish, and serve immediately.

Serves 3 to 4

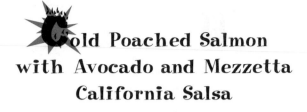

Cold Poached Salmon with Avocado and Mezzetta California Salsa

This refreshing salmon recipe is from G. L. Mezzetta. The combination of ingredients is unusual, and the finished dish is delightfully tangy. Serve this chilled entrée on a bed of mixed salad greens.

4 6-ounce salmon fillets
1 cup white wine
1/4 cup lemon juice
About 1/2 cup water
1 large, ripe avocado
1 cup *Mezzetta California Salsa*
  (or substitute B)
4 lemon slices

Place the salmon in a large skillet. Add the white wine, lemon juice, and enough water to cover the fillets. Poach the salmon until it is done, about 10 to 12 minutes. Remove the salmon from the pan and chill it.

Blend the avocado and the salsa until the mixture is smooth. Lay the chilled salmon on serving plates, and spoon the avocado sauce over it. Garnish with the lemon slices.

Serves 4

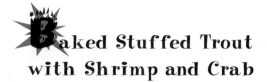aked Stuffed Trout with Shrimp and Crab

Chef Eddie Adams has created a seafood and fish extravaganza with this recipe that uses his Cajun Flavors Seafood Spice. Impress your guests with this rich, elegant dish, but don't tell them how easy it was to make!

6 tablespoons butter
1/2 cup chopped onion
2 garlic cloves, minced
1 tablespoon chopped green onions
1 tablespoon finely diced bell pepper
1/2 cup chopped celery
1/2 tablespoon *Eddie's Cajun Flavors Seafood Spice* (or substitute N)
1/2 cup bread crumbs
1 1/2 ounces dry white wine
1/2 cup cooked and chopped shrimp
1/2 cup chopped crab meat
2 tablespoons olive oil
Juice of 1 lemon
4 10-ounce whole trout, cleaned

Preheat the oven to 375 degrees.

In a pot, melt the butter. Sauté the onion, garlic, green onion, bell pepper, and celery for 2 minutes over medium heat. Add the remaining ingredients except the trout, and continue to cook for 3 minutes. Remove the mixture from the heat.

Stuff the trout with the mixture and wrap the trout with foil. Bake the trout for 10 minutes, then pull open the foil, and bake for an additional 5 minutes, or until the trout is done.

Serves 4

# Calamari Puttanesca

In Italian, puttanesca means "with harlot's sauce." It is quick and easy to make and was prepared between appointments. The Sauce of the Pirates is a rich, full sauce. We thank Dee Bronski and Mary Lee Wilcox, of Sumptuous Selections, for this recipe.

3 tablespoons olive oil
I garlic clove, chopped
I pound squid, cleaned and split lengthwise
I cup *Sumptuous Selections Sauce of the Pirates* (or substitute B)
2 cups penne or ziti pasta, cooked
I pound spinach, washed
3/4 cup bread crumbs

Heat the oil in a skillet.

Add the garlic, and then the squid. Sauté the squid.

Add the sauce and the pasta to the skillet, and toss to mix the ingredients. Immediately mix in the fresh raw spinach leaves. Transfer the mixture to a serving platter or bowls, top with the bread crumbs, and serve.

Serves 2

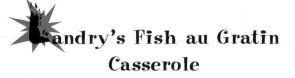# Landry's Fish au Gratin Casserole

If you are a catfish lover, this recipe is for you. We thank Scott Byron Landry of Byron's Catering, Lake Charles, Louisiana. The richness of the cheeses and the crunch of the broccoli provide contrast in this easy casserole.

I 1/2 pounds catfish
Byron's Seasoning, to taste (or substitute N)
I cup canned cheddar cheese soup
1/2 cup white wine
1/2 bag potato chips (8 ounces)
I cup grated Swiss cheese
I 3/4 cup broccoli florets or chopped broccoli
I cup sliced provolone cheese
I 1/4 cups grated cheddar cheese

Preheat the oven to 375 degrees.

Season the fish liberally with Byron's Seasoning. Lay the fish in a baking dish.

In a bowl, mix the soup and wine.

Crush the potato chips, and spread them over the fish. Pour half the soup and wine mixture over the fish and crushed chips.

Spread the Swiss cheese on top of the fish and soup mixture, then add the broccoli, provolone cheese, and the remaining soup mixture. Top with the cheddar cheese. Bake for 40 minutes or until the fish is white and flaky.

Serve the casserole hot.

Serves 3

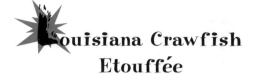ouisiana Crawfish Etouffée

Thanks to Chef Landry for this recipe for a Louisiana classic. He notes that you will need 6 1/2 pounds frozen crawfish to make 5 1/2 pounds drained weight. Serve the crawfish with cooked rice and a big green salad.

1/2 cup vegetable oil
1 cup flour
2 large yellow onions, chopped
2 large bell peppers, chopped
3/4 tablespoon garlic powder
1/2 cup tomato purée
1 quart boiling water
1/2 tablespoon ground black pepper
2 teaspoons salt
1/2 teaspoon cayenne powder
1 1/2 pounds thawed, if frozen,
  and drained crawfish tails
1/2 cup finely sliced green onion tops
1/2 cup chopped parsley

In a heavy pot, heat the oil to approximately 200 degrees. Add the flour, and cook about 10 minutes, stirring frequently until light brown.

Add the onions, peppers, garlic powder, and tomato purée, and simmer for 10 minutes.

Add the boiling water, black pepper, salt, and cayenne, and simmer for 15 minutes.

Add the crawfish, and simmer for 10 to 15 minutes.

Remove the pot from the heat, and stir in the green onions and parsley.

Serve the crawfish hot over rice.

Serves 3

Barbecued Shrimp Nawlins

Chef Eddie Adams offers for your pleasure a Louisiana-style shrimp dish containing one of his fine products. Serve this quick-to-prepare dish with a mixed salad and hot, crusty rolls.

3/4 pound butter
2 bay leaves
2 tablespoons *Eddie's Cajun Flavors Seafood Spice* (or substitute **N**)
1/4 cup chopped green onions
1/2 cup minced yellow onions
1/2 cup minced celery
5 garlic cloves, minced
1/4 cup beer
1/4 cup wine
Strained juice of 1 lemon
20 to 25 medium shrimp, cleaned, peeled, deveined, and cooked

In a 2-quart pot, melt the butter over medium-high heat. Add the next six ingredients. Sauté the mixture for 4 minutes, or until the vegetables are almost sticking to the pot.

Add the beer, wine, and lemon juice. Lower the heat, and cook approximately 4 minutes more, stirring occasionally. Pour the sauce over the shrimp and bake for 4 to 6 minutes. Or add the shrimp to the pot, and sauté them 2 minutes on each side.

Serve the shrimp hot.

Serves 4

Punished Scampi

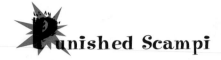

Hot Heads offers this hot and spicy shrimp dish, made with the company's Capital Punishment Sauce. Serve the shrimp over wild rice for an interesting combination of flavors.

1 1/2 teaspoon butter or margarine
1/4 cup diced green pepper
1/4 cup diced red onion
2 tablespoons white wine or light shrimp stock
16 to 20 medium shrimp, peeled and deveined
1/4 teaspoon *Capital Punishment Sauce* (or substitute **D** or **G**)
1/2 cup sliced mushrooms
4 thin lemon slices

Over high heat, melt the butter in a large skillet and sauté for 5 or 6 minutes the onion and pepper, stirring vigorously to brown. Add the wine and shrimp and the Capital Punishment Sauce and sauté. Keeping everything moving in the pan, add the mushrooms and lemon slices. When the shrimp are quite pink, serve the mixture over wild rice.

Serves 2 to 4

ili Shrimp

We thank GTL, Inc., for this tasty recipe. Not only is it quick to make, it is delicious to eat! Serve the shrimp with cooked rice and a green salad, with a creamy dressing.

1 pound jumbo shrimp, peeled
  and deveined
2 tablespoons *Pili Hot Pepper Condiment*
  (or substitute L)
2 tablespoons vegetable oil
1 green bell pepper, sliced in rounds
1 yellow bell pepper, sliced in rounds
1 red bell pepper, sliced in rounds
1 medium onion, thinly sliced in rounds
3 cups cooked rice

Marinate the shrimp in the Pili sauce for at least 30 minutes. Heat the oil in a large skillet or wok. When the oil begins to smoke, add the shrimp, and cook it approximately 1 1/2 minutes on each side. Remove the shrimp.

Sauté the peppers and onion in the same oil, until the onion is soft; the peppers should still be slightly crunchy. Spoon the peppers and onion over the rice, and top with the shrimp. Season with salt.

Serves 4

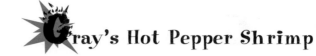ray's Hot Pepper Shrimp

Excelsior Trading Company is the distributor for the hot and spicy Gray's Products of Jamaica. In this dish from Excelsior, the cold, cooked shrimp seem to explode in your mouth with the hot and spicy flavors of the Scotch bonnets and Gray's Hot Pepper Sauce. Try these shrimp as an entrée or as an unusual appetizer.

3 tablespoons vegetable oil
3 tablespoons chopped fresh garlic
1 fresh Scotch bonnet chile, stemmed,
  seeded, and minced, or one teaspoon
  crushed dry Scotch bonnet chile
3 pounds jumbo shrimp, peeled and rinsed
1 tablespoon salt
1 tablespoon oyster sauce
1 tablespoon *Gray's Hot Pepper Sauce*
  (or substitute G)

In a large saucepan or wok, heat the oil. Add 1 tablespoon garlic and the Scotch bonnet. Sauté until the garlic is slightly brown.

Increase the heat, add the shrimp, and fry it until it is pink. Add the remaining ingredients, remove the mixture from the pan, and let cool.

Refrigerate the shrimp for at least 4 hours before serving.

Serves 4 to 6

Cajun Rush's Char-grilled Shrimp

This dish will conform to Healthy Heart Guidelines if you serve only three shrimp per person (instead of 6 or more). We thank Rush Biossat, the creator of Cajun Rush Pepper Sauce, for this great recipe. Serve the shrimp with cooked rice and a variety of steamed vegetables.

24 to 30 jumbo shrimp
1/4 cup *Cajun Rush Pepper Sauce*
(or substitute D)
1/2 cup grapefruit juice
3 tablespoons dried basil
2 tablespoons dried oregano
3/4 cup barbecue sauce
3 tablespoons chopped garlic
1/3 cup honey
1/4 cup olive or canola oil

Peel the shrimp, leaving on the tail section of the shell. Mix the remaining ingredients in a low-sided casserole or baking dish, and marinate the shrimp in the sauce for a few minutes.

Place the shrimp on a hot grill. After a minute or so, turn and baste them. Remove the shrimp from the grill as soon as they turn from translucent to white. (Watch carefully, as shrimp cooks quickly. Total cooking time should be no more than 2 to 3 minutes.) Baste the shrimp again, and serve them immediately.

The shrimp should be juicy and full of flavor.

Serves 4

Scallops Vero

Try this recipe for hot and spicy scallops. It comes highly recommended by Kim Wall of Sundance Foods, who likes to jazz up seafood by using her Sundance products—keeping the fat low and the spice high!

1 tablespoon canola oil
3 tablespoons butter or margarine
2 garlic cloves, crushed
1/2 pound mushrooms, sliced
1/2 cup dry sherry wine
1 tablespoon *Sundance All-Purpose*
Southwest Seasoning (or substitute A)
1 pound scallops, rinsed and drained

Heat a skillet, and melt the oil and butter or margarine. Lower the heat and sauté the garlic, taking care that it doesn't burn. Add the mushrooms, wine, and seasoning.

Turn the heat to high. Add the scallops, and sauté for 2 minutes. Reduce the heat to low, and cook for 2 minutes longer (do not overcook the scallops). Serve the scallops in individual bowls with the sauce.

Serves 4

Conch Chowder

Trish Jones, the Key West manufacturer of Big John's Famous Hot Sauce, sent us this information about her recipe: "Actually, you don't even need conch; it's tougher than rubber bands with just about as much flavor. But I like it. If you can't get conch, use ground pork and pretend that it's conch. As a matter of fact, conch is so expensive that it is a common occurrence in Key West to find ground pork in your conch chowder!"

2 tablespoons olive oil

2 large onions, sliced

2 large carrots, chopped

8 garlic cloves, crushed

2 tablespoons chile powder

2 tablespoons ground black pepper

2 tablespoons dried basil

2 tablespoons dried oregano

2 smoked ham hocks or hog jowls

1 cup tomato paste

2 cups canned whole tomatoes, drained
   (reserve the liquid)

1/2 cup beer

1/2 cup dry sherry

1/2 bottle *Big John's Hot Sauce*
   (or substitute **G**)

1 cup frozen corn

4 large potatoes, cubed

4 cups chicken broth

3 pounds conch, pounded and chopped,
   or ground pork

In a pot, heat the olive oil.

Sauté the onions, carrots, and garlic. Add the chile powder, pepper, basil, and oregano. When the vegetables are soft, put them in a crock pot.

Add the ham hocks or hog jowls, tomato paste, tomatoes, beer, sherry, liquid reserved from the tomatoes, hot sauce, corn, potatoes, and chicken broth, and bring the ingredients to a boil. Reduce the heat and simmer the mixture for 45 minutes. Add the conch or pork, and cook for another 4 to 6 hours.

Serve the chowder hot.

Serves 8 to 10

# Susie's Conch Salad

This recipe from Rosemarie McMaster of St. Johns, Antigua, uses her hot sauce, Susie's, and a favorite Caribbean shellfish, conch. Rosemarie's mother started the hot sauce company years ago, and Rosemarie has continued the family tradition.

3 pounds conch, cleaned and cut into long bite-size strips

1 tablespoon salt, for boiling the conch

1/4 cup vegetable oil

2 large red and yellow bell peppers, cut into long strips

3 sprigs thyme

3 bay leaves

3 medium onions, cut into long strips

1 garlic clove, crushed

3 celery sticks, diced

1 teaspoon Worcestershire sauce

4 teaspoons *Susie's Hot Sauce* (or substitute G)

Boil the conch in salted water until it is tender, about an hour, and drain it.

In a deep skillet, put the oil, bell peppers, thyme, bay leaves, onion, garlic, celery, Worcestershire sauce, and *Susie's Hot Sauce*, and sauté for 5 minutes, stirring constantly.

Add the conch. Sauté, stirring, for another 3 minutes.

Serve the mixture on a bed of lettuce, garnished with sliced tomatoes, cucumbers, and strips of red and yellow bell peppers.

Serves 6

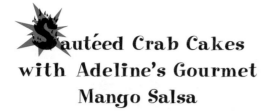

Sautéed Crab Cakes with Adeline's Gourmet Mango Salsa

Adeline Reyes is the creator of several exotic salsas a restaurant owner in Los Angeles, and her dishes don't stint on the heat! Her rich, spicy crab cakes literally melt in your mouth; they're so tender and hot.

2 tablespoons olive oil

1/2 cup chopped yellow onion

1/2 cup white wine

3/4 cup heavy cream

1/2 teaspoon diced Thai or serrano chile

2 teaspoons chopped chives

2 teaspoons chopped fresh dill

2 teaspoons chopped cilantro

1/2 teaspoon salt

1 large egg, lightly beaten

1 cup soft bread crumbs

1 1/4 pounds shelled crabmeat

2 tablespoons butter

2 to 4 tablespoons vegetable oil

2 cups *Adeline's Gourmet Mango Salsa*, warmed (or substitute J)

In a skillet, heat the olive oil. Sauté the onion with the wine until the onion is translucent, about 5 to 7 minutes. Transfer the mixture to a large bowl and let it cool.

In a small saucepan over low heat, reduce the cream with the chile until 1/2 cup remains. Let the mixture cool, then add the onion mixture. Stir in the chives, dill, cilantro, and salt. Stir in the egg and 1/2 cup bread crumbs. Gently fold in the crabmeat; the mixture will be lumpy. Divide the mixture into twelve crab cakes.

On a flat plate, spread the remaining 1/2 cup bread crumbs, and coat the crab cakes with them. Place the breaded cakes on a tray, and refrigerate them for 2 hours.

In a large skillet, melt the butter and vegetable oil. Sauté the crab cakes until they are golden brown on each side. Serve the hot crab cakes with the warmed salsa on top.

Serves 2

rabmeat Supreme

Chip Hearn, the creator of some fine hot sauces and the owner of Peppers and The Starboard Restaurant, has created this recipe of such spice and taste dimensions that people who taste it dream about having it again.

1/4 cup butter

3 tablespoons all-purpose flour

1/2 cup heavy cream

1/2 cup milk

Salt and pepper to taste

I cup mayonnaise

1/2 teaspoon salt

I egg

I tablespoon Worcestershire sauce

2 teaspoons *Hot Bitch at the Beach* hot sauce (or substitute D)

2 pounds crabmeat

2 cups soft bread crumbs

I 1/2 teaspoons paprika

1/2 teaspoon garlic salt

2 tablespoons melted butter

1/2 pound cooked bacon, crumbled

Preheat the oven to 400 degrees.

Melt the butter in a skillet, add the flour and stir to make a roux. Add the cream and milk and heat, but do not boil. Add the mayonnaise, salt, egg, Worcestershire sauce, and Hot Bitch at the Beach hot sauce. Lightly stir the mixture until it is blended.

Fold in the crabmeat, and gently pour the mixture into a greased casserole dish.

Blend the bread crumbs, paprika, and garlic salt together, and cover the crab mixture with the crumbs. Sprinkle the casserole with the melted butter and crumbled bacon. Bake the casserole for 20 minutes, and serve it hot.

Serves 4 to 6

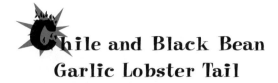

Chile and Black Bean Garlic Lobster Tail

If you like lobster, you'll love this recipe from Lee Kum Kee. It adds to lobster more spice, heat, and flavor than you've ever known before. Serve the lobster with rice, sautéed snow peas and water chestnuts, and crisp rice cakes.

**2 pounds lobster tails, cut into
    desired sizes**
2 tablespoons cornstarch (optional)
2 tablespoons vegetable oil, for frying
2 1/2 tablespoons *Lee Kum Kee Black Bean
    Garlic Sauce* **(or substitute M)**
1 teaspoon minced ginger
2 green onions, sliced
**1 jalapeño, stemmed, seeded, and sliced
    into strips**
1 tablespoon *Panda Brand Sriracha Chili
    Sauce* **(or substitute L)**
1 tablespoon *Lee Kum Kee Chicken
    Marinade* **(or substitute M)**
1 1/2 teaspoons sugar

Rinse and dry the lobster meat. Coat the meat with the cornstarch, if you prefer. Deep-fry the meat in hot oil for 1 minute. Drain it, and set it aside.

Heat a large, heavy skillet, and add about 2 tablespoons oil. Sauté the black bean-garlic sauce and the ginger. Add the lobster, and cook, stirring until it is half done. Add the remaining ingredients, and stir-fry well.

Serve the lobster hot with steamed rice.

Serves 4

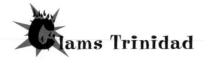

Clams Trinidad

Thank you to Caribbean Food Products for this delicious and easy-to-prepare recipe! The herbs in the Trinidad Habanero Pepper Sauce really stand out in this wonderful clam dish. Serve it with fettucine Alfredo and sliced fresh tomatoes.

1/3 cup butter

2 cups chopped onions

1 cup chopped green bell pepper

6 crumbled slices cooked bacon

1/2 cup grated Parmesan cheese

4 to 5 teaspoons *Trinidad Habanero Pepper Sauce* (or substitute G)

2 to 3 dozen steamed fresh clams, on half shells

Preheat the oven to 350 degrees.

In a skillet, melt the butter. Sauté the onions and bell peppers until they are soft. Add the bacon, cheese, and pepper sauce. Cover the steamed clams with the mixture. Bake the clams for 10 minutes, and serve them hot.

Serves 4

Power Pastas
and Galvanized Grains

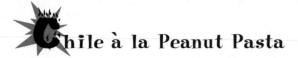Chile à la Peanut Pasta

This recipe, from Stacy Tanner of Bowman's Landing Epicurean Company, is easy to prepare and combines some interesting flavors and textures. If you like, add 2 cups cooked cubed chicken breasts to the cooked pasta.

1/4 cup *Jazzy Ginger Vinegar*
  (or substitute C)
8 large pinches sugar
1/4 cup peanut oil
2 tablespoons smooth peanut butter
1 bag *Chile Peanut Pasta* (or substitute T)
1 medium cucumber, seeded and chopped
1 cup salted skinless peanuts,
  coarsely chopped
1/4 cup chopped chives
1/4 teaspoon dried red pepper flakes

In a bowl, make the sauce by combining the Jazzy Ginger Vinegar, sugar, peanut oil, and peanut butter. Mix until the sauce is smooth. Set the sauce aside.

Cook and drain the pasta. While the pasta is hot, add the cucumber, peanuts, chives, red pepper, and sauce. Toss the pasta, and serve it immediately.

Serves 4 to 6

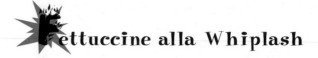Fettuccine alla Whiplash

Many thanks to Tom Hill of Chef's Choice for this recipe which contains his spicy marinade and blending sauce, Whiplash. The fettuccine is rich, creamy, and spicy. Add a salad with an oil-and-vinegar dressing, and dinner is ready.

Alfredo Sauce:
1 cup heavy cream
1/2 cup grated PARMESAN cheese
2 tablespoons butter
1 egg yolk

2 tablespoons butter
1/2 clove garlic
1 cup fresh broccoli florets, steamed
  and drained
1/4 cup *Whiplash Sauce*
  (or substitute D)
6 ounces fettuccine noodles, cooked
  al dente

Make the Alfredo sauce: In a saucepan, heat the cream. Add the cheese and butter, stir, and heat until the mixture is creamy; do not allow it to boil. Stir in the egg yolk, and blend well. Remove the pan from the heat.

Melt the butter in a saucepan, and lightly sauté the garlic and broccoli. Add the Whiplash sauce. Gently fold the ingredients into the pasta, and top with the Alfredo sauce.

Serve the pasta at once.

Serves 2 to 3

ajun Hot Pasta

We thank Stan and Bruci Gauthier, of La Cour de la Ferme, for this hot and spicy recipe which reflects their hot and spicy Louisiana roots. For variety, you can add shrimp, sausage to the pasta. or whatever else your taste buds are crying out for.

6 ounces pasta of your choice
1/4 cup olive oil
2 teaspoons dried basil, crushed
1/4 teaspoon dried oregano
1/8 teaspoon dried thyme
2 teaspoons chopped garlic
2 tablespoons *T-Loui's Cajun Chow Chow* (or substitute H)
2 ounces dried tomatoes, sliced
1 medium yellow squash, sliced thin
1 medium zucchini, sliced thin
8 ounces mushrooms, sliced thin
1 1/2 tablespoons *Andre's Rouge* (spiced Cajun hot sauce) (or substitute G)
1 tablespoon *Pee Wee's Cajun Cayenne Juice* (or substitute D)
2 teaspoons *Pont Breaux Cajun Powder* (or substitute N)
2 ounces pimentos, sliced
1 tablespoon balsamic vinegar
1/4 cup grated Parmesan cheese

Cook the pasta according to the package directions. Drain the pasta, rinse it, and set it aside.

In a pot, heat the olive oil over medium heat. Sauté the basil, oregano, thyme, garlic, chow chow, and tomatoes in the olive oil for approximately 5 minutes.

Add the yellow squash, zucchini, mushrooms, spiced Cajun hot sauce, cayenne juice, and Cajun powder, and stir. Add the pimentos and balsamic vinegar, and cook for another 3 to 4 minutes, stirring occasionally.

Add the pasta and stir carefully to avoid breaking the pieces. Cover the pot, and continue cooking for approximately 3 to 4 minutes. Add the Parmesan cheese, toss the pasta, and serve immediately.

Serves 6 to 8

lazin' High Noon Pasta

Thanks to Tim Fex of Blazin' Oregon Food Products for this recipe. His Blazin' Oregon Hot Hazelnuts add both texture and heat to this pasta.

1 1/2 teaspoons canola oil

1/2 cup diced red onion

1 cup coarsely chopped wild mushrooms

2 garlic cloves, finely minced

3 to 4 Italian tomatoes, peeled, seeded, and chopped

3 to 4 tomatillos, blackened in a skillet and chopped

1 to 2 jalapeño chiles, stemmed, seeded, and diced

1/2 teaspoon cumin, toasted and ground

1/4 teaspoon dried Mexican oregano

2 to 3 chiltepin chiles, crushed (optional)

1/2 cup finely chopped *Blazin' Oregon Hot Hazelnuts* (or substitute E)

1/2 cup chicken broth

Salt and pepper to taste

1/4 cup finely grated dry jack cheese

1/2 pound fresh linguine (red pepper linguine is especially good), cooked and drained

In a saucepan, heat the canola oil. Sauté the onion until it is limp. Add the mushrooms, and cook over a medium heat until the mushrooms are half done (about 1 minute).

Add the garlic and stir briefly. Then add the tomatoes, tomatillos, jalapeños, cumin, oregano, and chiltepins. Cook until the tomatoes begin to collapse, about 2 minutes. Add three-fourths of the hazelnuts (reserve the larger pieces for a garnish) and add 1/4 cup chicken broth. Cook the sauce to a medium consistency, thinning with more chicken broth if necessary. Add salt and pepper to taste.

Pour the sauce over the hot pasta, and top with the grated cheese. Garnish with the remaining hazelnuts.

Serves 2

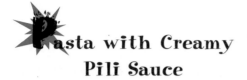

Pasta with Creamy Pili Sauce

We thank GTL, Inc., for this recipe. Since the Pili Hot Pepper Condiment contains habanero chiles, this pasta dish has the distinctive habanero flavor and heat, which is tempered by the tomatoes and the cream.

6 medium fresh tomatoes, peeled
   (or 2 cups canned tomatoes)
3 tablespoons butter
3 tablespoons *Pili Hot Pepper Condiment*
   (or substitute L)
1 1/2 tablespoons all-purpose flour
1 cup half-and-half
Salt to taste
1 pound fusilli or rigatoni pasta, cooked
   and drained

Purée the tomatoes in a blender.

Melt 1 tablespoon butter in a saucepan. Add the Pili condiment, and sauté it over medium heat for 1 minute. Add the tomatoes, and simmer for 15 minutes.

While the tomatoes simmer, melt the remaining 2 tablespoons butter in a separate saucepan. Add the flour, and cook until the roux is golden, stirring constantly with a whisk. Heat the cream (do not let it boil) on the stove or in a microwave oven. Add the hot cream to the flour mixture, and cook, stirring over low heat until the mixture thickens.

Combine the cream and tomato mixtures. Season with salt. Spoon the sauce over the hot pasta, and serve immediately.

Serves 4 to 6

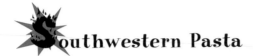

Southwestern Pasta

Thank you to Hunter-McKenzie and the McIlhenny Company for this winning recipe. The punch of the Tabasco sauce contrasts nicely with the cilantro in the pasta sauce. Serve the pasta with a big green salad, dressed with a creamy dressing.

1/4 cup olive oil

2 medium onions, sliced

1 garlic clove, minced

3 1/2 cups peeled tomatoes, crushed

3/4 teaspoon *Tabasco Pepper Sauce*
   (or substitute D)

1/4 teaspoon salt

2-3 tablespoons minced fresh cilantro

1/4 teaspoon sugar

12 ounces angel's hair pasta, cooked
   and drained

Heat the oil over medium heat in a large, heavy, nonreactive saucepan. Stir in the onions and garlic, sauté for 10 to 12 minutes, stirring occasionally, until the onions are tender.

Add the tomatoes, Tabasco sauce, salt, cilantro, and sugar, and bring the mixture to a boil. Reduce the heat to low, and simmer the mixture, uncovered, for 30 minutes or until it is slightly thickened.

Place the hot cooked pasta on a heated serving platter, and top with the sauce. Sprinkle the pasta, if you like, with grated Parmesan cheese.

Serves 4

Angel Hair Pasta with Shrimp, Tomato and Pikled Garlik Salza

Judy Knapp of The Pikled Garlik Company has given us this recipe, which uses two of her fine products. If you have never tasted pickled garlic, treat yourself to this addictive delight! Its use in this pasta dish is a real palate-pleaser.

1 tablespoon vegetable oil

3 cloves *Red Chili Pikled Garlik*
   (or substitute fresh garlic)

1 fresh tomato, cut in half, squeezed to
   remove excess liquid and seeds, and
   coarsely chopped

1/2 cup medium shrimp, cleaned and
   cooked

6 tablespoons *Pikled Garlik Company Salza*
   (or substitute B)

1/2 pound angel's hair pasta, cooked
   and drained

Heat the oil in a small pan. Sauté the garlic for 1 minute, and then add the tomato. Cook over low heat for 5 minutes. Add the shrimp and salsa, and continue cooking just long enough to heat the shrimp through.

Toss the sauce with the hot pasta, and serve.

Serves 2 to 3

picy Fried Rice

Laura Deck of The Great Southwest Spice Company has devised this tasty, quick recipe using one of her many fine products. The rice is a great accompaniment for chicken, beef, or lamb.

1/4 cup vegetable oil or margarine
1 medium yellow onion, chopped
1 large green pepper, thinly sliced
1 large red pepper, thinly sliced
4 cups cooked rice
1/4 cup *Great Southwest All-Purpose Chili Seasoning* (or substitute O)

Heat the oil or margarine in a large skillet, and sauté the vegetables for 5 minutes. Add the rice and seasoning. Cook for 15 minutes, stirring continuously. Serve the rice hot.

Serves 2 to 4

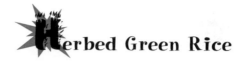erbed Green Rice

The combination of all the herbs and the dill-flavored vinegar makes this rice dish from Spirit Mesa most refreshing. Try the rice with fish, cold meats, or spicy barbecued ribs.

1/2 cup long-grain rice, cooked
Salt and pepper to taste
3 tablespoons olive oil
2 teaspoons *Spirit Mesa Dill Vinegar* (or substitute C)
Squeeze of lemon juice
2 tablespoons chopped parsley
2 tablespoons chopped chives
1 tablespoon chopped dill
1 tablespoon chopped tarragon

While the rice is still hot, stir in the salt, pepper, oil, vinegar, and lemon juice. When the rice has cooled, slightly stir in the chopped herbs, and serve.

Serves 2 to 4

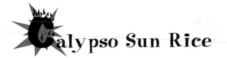 **Calypso Sun Rice**

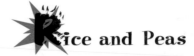 **Rice and Peas**

Rica Red Calypso Sun Sauce unites papayas with habanero chiles to produce a sweet and hot sauce that combines well with any number of fruits. For this rice we mix the sauce with raisins, bananas, coconut, and shrimp for a tasty side dish or, if more shrimp is added, an entrée. Thanks to Los Dos for this tropical recipe.

1/4 cup minced onion

2 tablespoons butter or margarine

1 cup small shrimp

1 cup raw rice

1 1/2 cups chicken broth

1/2 cup coconut milk

1/4 cup *Rica Red Calypso Sun Sauce*
  (or substitute J)

1/2 cup golden raisins

1/4 cup chopped bananas

1/4 cup toasted coconut

2 tablespoons chopped cilantro

In a skillet, melt the butter. Sauté the onion until it is soft. Add the shrimp, and sauté for 1 minute. Stir in the rice, and continue to sauté until the rice turns opaque. Remove the pan from the heat.

In a saucepan, bring the broth, coconut milk, and Calypso Sun Sauce to a boil. Add the rice, and bring the mixture back to a boil. Stir in the raisins, reduce the heat, cover the pot, and simmer for 20 to 30 minutes, or until the rice is done.

Remove the pan from the heat, add the bananas, coconut, and cilantro, and serve.

Serves 4

Coconut milk is used frequently in the West Indies, in various dishes. The red pea referred to in this recipe may be better recognized as the kidney bean. We thank Island Imports, the creator of Evadney's products, for this great Caribbean recipe. Try serving rice and peas with hot and spicy curry dishes.

4 cups canned coconut milk

2 cups dry red peas (kidney beans)

1 sprig fresh thyme

3 tablespoons *Evadney's All Purpose*
  Hot Sauce (or substitute G)

1 garlic clove, crushed

1 scallion, chopped

Salt and pepper to taste

2 cups raw rice

Put the coconut milk into a saucepan. Add the red peas. Boil the mixture covered until the red peas are tender. 1-2 hours.

Add the thyme, hot sauce, garlic, scallion, and salt and pepper to the red peas. Simmer for 2 minutes. Add the rice; the liquid should cover it by about 1 inch. Bring the mixture to a boil, cover the pan, and turn the heat to low. Simmer until the liquid disappears and the rice is fully cooked.

Serves 6 to 8

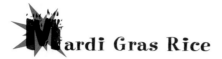ardi Gras Rice

We thank La Cour de la Ferme for this recipe for a delicious and colorful rice dish. The aroma that the dish exudes when it is cooking really alerts the taste buds. Try serving the rice with grilled fish or chicken.

4 tablespoons butter or margarine

2 bunches green onions, green and white parts sliced separately

1 tablespoon minced garlic

3 stalks celery, chopped

1 medium yellow onion, chopped

1/4 medium red onion, chopped

1/2 medium red bell pepper, chopped

1/2 medium green bell pepper, chopped

1/2 medium yellow bell pepper, chopped

1 tablespoon *T-Loui's Cajun Chow Chow* (or substitute L)

1/4 cup *Pee Wee's Cajun Cayenne Juice* (or substitute D)

1/2 tablespoon *Andre's Rouge* (spiced Cajun hot sauce) (or substitute D)

1/2 tablespoon *Pont Breaux Cajun Powder* (or substitute N)

2 1/2 cups raw long-grain rice

3 cups chicken broth

In a skillet over a medium heat, melt the margarine. Sauté the white parts of the green onions with the garlic, celery, onions, bell peppers, and chow chow until the vegetables are wilted (approximately 15 minutes).

Put the wilted ingredients into a rice cooker or large saucepan, along with the cayenne juice, spiced Cajun hot sauce, cajun powder, rice, chicken broth, and green onion tops. Cook the rice according to the rice cooker directions, or bring the ingredients to a boil in the saucepan, cover the pan, and reduce the heat. Steam the rice covered, until it is done, and serve it hot.

Serves 10 to 12

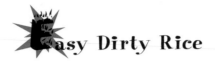

Easy Dirty Rice

Dirty rice, a Cajun specialty, is named for the addition of meat—often ground giblets—to the rice. This recipe from La Cour de la Ferme, created by Stan and Bruci Gauthier, uses many of their fine Cajun products. You will love it, we guarantee.

1 pound lean ground beef

1 pound lean ground pork

1 teaspoon paprika

1 teaspoon dry mustard

1 1/2 medium onions, chopped

1 1/2 medium green bell peppers, chopped

3 celery stalks, chopped

2 tablespoons minced garlic

2 bunches green onions, green and white parts sliced separately

1 tablespoon *T-Loui's Cajun Chow Chow* (or substitute H)

1 tablespoon *Pee Wee's Cajun Cayenne Juice* (or substitute D)

2 1/2 tablespoons *Andre's Rouge* (spiced Cajun hot sauce) (or substitute D)

1 tablespoon *Pont Breaux Cajun Powder* (or substitute N)

1 1/4 cups cream of celery soup

1 1/4 cups French onion soup

2 cups raw long-grain rice

1 1/2 cups water

In an ovenproof skillet over medium heat, brown the beef and pork, stirring as needed to prevent sticking. Drain the meat of excess fat. Add the paprika, mustard, onions, bell peppers, celery, garlic, white parts of the green onions, chow chow, cayenne juice, spiced Cajun hot sauce, and Cajun powder. Stir well. Continue cooking for approximately 5 minutes, stirring as needed to avoid sticking.

Add the celery soup and onion soup, stir well, cover the pan and continue cooking until the mixture begins to bubble. Add the rice and green onion tops, stir well, and remove the pan from the heat. Add the 1 1/2 cups water. If the rice is not completely covered by the liquid, add more water. Cover the pan, and place the pan in a 350 degree F oven for 45 minutes. Check the rice occasionally; if the mixture appears dry, add water, and resume baking until the rice is tender and moist.

Serve the rice hot.

Serves 8 to 10

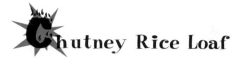

Chutney Rice Loaf

Tadd Mick of Mick's Peppourri devised this unusual and tasty rice loaf, enhanced by apple chutney and pecans. If you omit the meat, this makes a great side dish for a spicy curry dinner.

I cup soft bread crumbs
I cup cooked rice
3 eggs, beaten
I cup *Mick's Apple Chutney*
  (or substitute U)
I cup chopped pecans
I 1/2 cups milk
2 cups chopped chicken or other meat

Preheat the oven to 350 degrees.

Combine all of the ingredients, and pour them into a greased loaf pan. Bake the loaf for I hour.

Turn the loaf out of the pan onto a serving platter. Serve the loaf with chicken or beef gravy.

Serves 6 to 8

Achiote Pork and Beans

Achiote Indian Sauce gives this dish a unique flavor. We thank Hot Heads, Inc., for this great recipe.

I medium onion, diced
I carrot, diced
2 strips bacon, diced
1/4 cup *Achiote Indian Sauce*
  (or substitute B)
I pork tenderloin, cut into 1/2-inch cubes
I cup cooked pinto beans
1/2 cup water

Preheat the oven to 325 degrees.

In a large casserole, lightly sauté the onion, carrots, and bacon together, and then add the Achiote sauce. Add the pork, and stir a little. Then add the prepared beans and the water, and cover the dish. Bake for 45 minutes to I hour.

Serve the pork and beans hot.

Serves 4

Corn Chip Pie

Joy's Party Wheel

Thanks to Mangum Enterprises for this fast and spicy side dish. Served with a big salad, it could be a complete meal. It is also good with grilled burgers or chicken.

2 cups corn chips
I cup grated cheddar cheese
I cup chili con carne
I cup cooked pinto beans
  or black beans
I cup chopped New Mexican green chile

Spread the corn chips in a 9- by 13-inch pan. Sprinkle the cheddar cheese over the corn chips. Combine the chili con carne, pinto beans, and green chile in a saucepan and heat. Pour this mixture over the corn chips and cheese. Serve the pie while it is hot, with a lettuce, tomato, and avocado salad.

Serves 4

This recipe is great for parties because it can be made ahead of time and refrigerated until needed. We thank Joy's of Colorado for this interesting taste creation, which uses one of Joy's fine products, Chimayo Red Chile Jelly.

2 cups refried beans, room temperature
1/2 jar *Chimayo Red Chile Jelly*
  (or substitute K)
3 avocados, peeled and pitted
1/2 teaspoon salt
1/4 teaspoon ground black pepper
2 tablespoons lemon juice
I package taco seasoning mix
1/2 cup mayonnaise
I cup sour cream
3 green onions, chopped
2 tomatoes, chopped
I small can sliced black olives
1/2 pound colby or longhorn cheese, grated

Spread the refried beans on a large, flat serving dish, and spread the chile jelly on top of beans.

In a bowl, mash the avocados and mix in the salt, pepper, and lemon juice. Spread this mixture over the beans and jelly.

In another bowl, mix the taco seasoning, mayonnaise, and sour cream. Spread this mixture on the avocado mixture. Top with the green onions, tomatoes, black olives, and cheese.

Serve the wheel with chips.

Serves 4 to 6

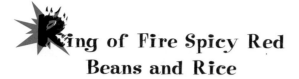

Ring of Fire Spicy Red Beans and Rice

Thanks to the folks who manufacture Ring of Fire Hot Sauce for this recipe. We like to prepare this dish on weekends, preferably when it's raining or snowing because the rich aroma fills and warms the house. The special hot sauce in the recipe brings a warmth to your mouth, too.

2 cups dried red beans
2 medium ham hocks
12 cups water
1 tablespoon butter
4 chopped garlic cloves
1 large yellow onion, diced
3/4 cup chopped celery
1 teaspoon dried thyme, or
 1 tablespoon fresh
2 bay leaves
1 pound andouille sausage, diced
2 cups peeled tomatoes
1/2 cup *Ring of Fire Hot Sauce*
 (or substitute D)
1/2 teaspoon liquid smoke flavoring
 (optional)
2 cups hot cooked rice

Soak the beans overnight.

In a large pot, bring the water and the ham hocks to a simmer. In a skillet, melt the butter. Add the garlic, onion, celery, thyme, and bay leaves. Sauté for approximately 5 minutes, until the onion and celery are soft. Add the vegetable mixture to the pot with the ham hocks, and simmer for 30 minutes. Add the soaked beans and sausage, and simmer for 1 1/2 hours, stirring occasionally and adding water if needed.

Add the tomatoes, Ring of Fire Hot Sauce, and, if you like, liquid smoke, and simmer for another 1 1/2 hours.

Remove the ham hocks and bay leaves before serving. Serve the red beans over the rice.

Serves 4 to 6

Saguaro's Black Bean Tostadas with Baked Tortillas

We thank the Saguaro Potato Chip Company of Tucson for providing this recipe. The combination of creamy and crisp ingredients on the tortillas is very refreshing. Serve these tostadas alone for a light lunch (the salad is on the top) or along with a grilled burger or chicken breast topped with one of those great Saguaro Salsas. (By the way, The Saguaro Company also makes excellent flavored potato chips.)

8 corn tortillas
1 1/2 cups cold water
Saguaro's No-Fat Black Bean Dip
  (or substitute other bean dip)
1/2 head iceberg lettuce, shredded
5 green onions, chopped
3 tablespoons chopped cilantro
2 cups shredded reduced-fat jack cheese
1 large tomato, chopped
1 small avocado, diced
Saguaro's Southwest Salsa to taste
  (or substitute B)
Saguaro's Chipotle Salsa to taste
  (or substitute B)

Preheat the oven to 350 degrees.

Dip the tortillas in cold water, and drain them on paper towels. Place the tortillas on the oven rack, and bake them for 15 minutes or until they are crisp.

Remove the tortillas from the oven, and let them cool.

When the tortillas are cooled, layer each with the bean dip, lettuce, green onion, cilantro, cheese, tomato, avocado, and salsa. Serve immediately.

Serves 4

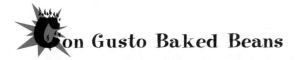

Con Gusto Baked Beans

From the heart of chile country, Las Cruces, New Mexico, comes this super-fast, super-good recipe from Lisa Asel of the Ol' Gringo Chile Products Company. These beans are sweet, hot, and spicy, and such a change from the ordinary baked beans. Make this dish for your next cookout, and watch people take seconds.

4 cups cooked pinto beans
1 medium onion, diced
1/2 cup brown sugar
14 teaspoon ground cumin
1/4 teaspoon dried oregano
1/2 teaspoon garlic salt
1 cup *Ol' Gringo Red Chile Sauce*
  (or substitute B)

Preheat the oven to 350 degrees.

Combine the ingredients in a casserole, and bake for 25 minutes.

Serve the beans hot. They are a great barbecue accompaniment.

Serves 4 to 6

Zack's Grit Fritters

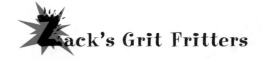

Thanks to Zack's Foods for this delicious, tongue-tingling recipe. Serve these fritters at your next barbecue with some hot and spicy meat and some creamy coleslaw, or for brunch with a fruit salad and scrambled eggs (or shirred eggs with a drop or two of Zack's hot sauce on top).

1 cup all-purpose flour
1 teaspoon salt
1 teaspoon baking soda
1 egg
1 teaspoon chopped chives
1/4 cup grated cheddar cheese
1 cup cold cooked grits
1/2 cup finely chopped ham
1/2 teaspoon *Zack's Virgin Habanero Sauce*
  (or substitute G)
1/4 cup vegetable oil

Mix together all of the ingredients except the oil, and refrigerate the mixture, covered, overnight.

Heat the oil, and shape the mixture into patties. Cook the fritters over a medium heat for 2 to 4 minutes per side. Serve them hot.

Serves 2

Spiced Black Bean Soup

The Virgin Islands Herb and Pepper Company contributed this delicious soup recipe. We like the tropical tastes of the rum and the hot sauce in this dish. Serve this along with something Caribbean style from your grill.

1 cup dry black beans
6 cups water
4 slices bacon
1 medium onion, chopped
1 garlic clove, minced
2 cups tomato sauce
2 teaspoons salt
1/2 teaspoon dried and crushed oregano
2 tablespoons *Mountain Herb Hot Sauce*
  (or substitute **G**)
1/2 cup rum
Lemon or lime slices, for garnish

In a 3-quart saucepan, combine the beans and water, and soak the beans overnight.

Do not drain the beans. Simmer them covered, for 2 1/2 to 3 hours, or until the beans are tender.

In a small skillet, cook the bacon until it is crisp. Drain the bacon, and reserve 2 tablespoons of the drippings. Crumble the bacon, and set it aside.

Sauté the onion and garlic in the reserved drippings until they are tender. Add the sautéed mixture to the beans along with the tomato sauce, salt, oregano, and 2 tablespoons Mountain Herb Hot Sauce. Cover the pan, and simmer for 30 minutes. Purée the bean mixture in batches in a blender. Return the puréed beans to the saucepan and stir in the rum. Heat the beans thoroughly, for 5 to 10 minutes.

Serve the beans garnished with the crumbled bacon and lemon or lime slices. Serve additional hot sauce on the side.

Serves 4 to 6

Sensational Side Dishes

Double-Baked Potato Baptized in Rio Diablo

Rio Diablo contributed this zesty recipe to our collection. The stuffed potato is a great accompaniment to any entrée.

1 large baking potato
Salt and pepper to taste
1 tablespoon sliced black olives
2 teaspoons *Rio Diablo Salsa*
  (or substitute B)
1/3 cup extra sharp cheddar cheese, grated
1 1/2 tablespoons sour cream

Bake the potato at 375 degrees for 1 hour or until it is tender when pierced with a fork. Leave the oven on.

Let the potato cool slightly, then cut it in half lengthwise. Scrape out the pulp without tearing the skin, and put the pulp into a bowl. Salt and pepper the potato skin halves, and set them aside. Mash the potato pulp, and stir in the sliced olives, the salsa, 1/3 cup cheese, and the sour cream. Fill the potato skin halves with the mixture, and top with the remaining cheese. Bake the potato for another 15 minutes, and serve it hot.

Serves 2

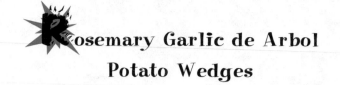

Rosemary Garlic de Arbol Potato Wedges

These potatoes are a tasty, spicy accompaniment to roast pork, beef, and chicken. They require Los Dos products, chile de arbol powder and Rick's Desert Devil Oil, an extra-virgin olive oil flavored with both black and red peppers.

3 tablespoons *Rick's Desert Devil Oil*
  (or substitute S)
3 to 4 garlic cloves, minced
1 tablespoon chopped fresh rosemary
  or dried rosemary
3 to 4 large potatoes, cut into wedges
1/4 teaspoon *Los Dos Gourmet Chile de Arbol Powder* (or substitute chile powder)
Salt to taste

Preheat the oven to 350 degrees.

Heat the oil in a small skillet. Saute the garlic cloves in the oil until they start to brown. Remove the garlic, and stir the rosemary into the oil. Remove the pan from the heat.

Place the potatoes in a baking pan, pour the oil over the top, sprinkle with the chile de arbol powder, and season with salt. Bake the potatoes for an hour, or until the potatoes are golden and crispy.

Serve the potatoes hot.

Serves 4 to 6

Corn Medley

Try this crunchy, fresh side dish at your next cookout. The dish travels well to a picnic, and the flavors go well with just about any kind of meat. Thanks to Wayne Doerr of The Alder Market for this recipe, and for creating his positively addicting salad dressings!

I cup fresh, canned, or frozen corn kernels
I small zucchini, diced small
1/2 small red onion, diced small
1/2 medium red pepper, diced small
I small ripe tomato, diced small
2 jalapeño chiles, stemmed, seeded,
   and minced
1/2 cup *Alder Market Spinach Salad Dressing*
   (or substitute other salad dressing
   with red wine vinegar)
Salt and pepper to taste

Cook and drain the corn. Place the corn in a bowl, and add the remaining ingredients. Stir the mixture together, and add salt and pepper to taste.

Serves 6 to 8

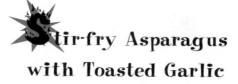

Stir-fry Asparagus with Toasted Garlic

The garlic in this recipe is sautéed in the oil until it is very brown. When drained and crumbled over the asparagus, the garlic almost tastes like nuts. Rick's Desert Devil Oil and Island Soy Sauce, both from Los Dos, give the vegetables subtle heat.

I pound fresh asparagus
6 garlic cloves, thinly sliced
2 tablespoons *Rick's Desert Devil Oil*
   (or substitute S)
I teaspoon grated fresh ginger
3 green onions, chopped
I tablespoon *Island Soy Sauce*
   (or substitute other soy sauce)

Cut the asparagus diagonally into 1 1/2-inch lengths. Blanch the asparagus in boiling water for 30 seconds, then immediately plunge it into ice water to stop the cooking.

Heat the oil in a small skillet. Sauté the garlic until it is quite brown. Remove the garlic and reserve it. Add the ginger to the pan, and stir-fry it for 30 seconds. Add the asparagus and green onions, and stir-fry for 1 minute. Stir in the soy sauce, and stir-fry for 2 minutes or until the asparagus is done but still crisp.

Crumble the garlic on top of the asparagus, and serve.

Serves 4

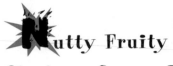utty Fruity Chutney Casserole

This recipe, from Tadd and Rod Mick of Mick's Peppourri, has a melange of tastes and ingredients, and it makes a flavorful addition to a meal of grilled fish or chicken. A family-run business, Mick's Peppourri also produces premium jellies.

I 1/2 cups fresh or frozen broccoli
I cup *Mick's Apple Chutney*
   (or substitute U)
1/2 cup nonfat salad dressing
2 eggs, well beaten
I cup chopped pecans
I cup shredded sharp cheddar cheese
I cup dry bread crumbs

Combine the broccoli, chutney, salad dressing, eggs, and pecans in a 2-quart greased casserole dish. Sprinkle the cheese and bread crumbs on top and bake for 30 minutes.

Serve the casserole hot.

Serves 6 to 8

Spicy Okra with Garlic and Tomatoes

When tomatoes first were brought to the Old World, they were thought to be poisonous and to have aphrodisiac qualities. Busha Brown Love Apple Sauce derives its name from that time when the French called tomatoes *pommes d'amour*; Love Apple Sauce is actually a tomato sauce. This delicious recipe will having you eating okra even if you thought you didn't like it.

2 tablespoons olive oil
I large onion, chopped fine
4 garlic cloves, crushed
5 large tomatoes, peeled and chopped
2 tablespoons *Busha Browne's Love Apple Sauce* (or substitute B)
2 tablespoons chopped fresh basil
I teaspoon salt
Freshly ground black pepper to taste
I pound okra, trimmed
1/2 fresh Scotch bonnet chile, stemmed, seeded, and chopped (optional)
Whole basil leaves, for garnish

Heat the olive oil in a large saucepan. Lightly sauté the onion and garlic; do not let the garlic brown. Stir in the tomatoes, Love Apple Sauce, basil, salt, and pepper. Add the okra, and simmer for 15 to 20 minutes, depending on the size of the pods. Add the Scotch bonnet chile, if you like. Serve the okra garnished with whole basil leaves.

Serves 4

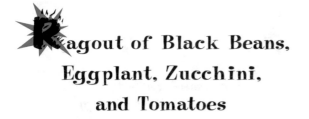agout of Black Beans, Eggplant, Zucchini, and Tomatoes

Cilantro, also known as coriander, was believed by the Chinese to confer immortality. Spirit Mesa manufactures cilantro vinegar and many fine herbal vinegars as well as other products, and we thank them for this terrific vegetable dish. If you have a summer garden, then this recipe is a natural.

2 tablespoons vegetable oil
1 small eggplant, cubed
1 small red bell pepper, seeded and cut into squares
2 jalapeño chiles, stemmed, seeded and diced
1 medium onion, cut into 1/2-inch pieces
3 large garlic cloves, minced
1 rounded tablespoon ground cumin
2 medium zucchini, cut into 1/2-inch cubes
4 cups cooked black beans (if they are canned, rinse and drain them)
2 cups Italian tomatoes, blended
1/4 cup *Spirit Mesa Cilantro Vinegar* (or substitute C)
2 tablespoons parsley, chopped
Salt to taste

Heat the oil in a large pot. Sauté the eggplant, red bell pepper, jalapeños, and onion in the oil for 10 minutes, stirring frequently. Add the garlic, and sauté for 1 minute. Add the cumin and zucchini, and sauté for 5 minutes. Add the beans, tomatoes, and vinegar; cover the pot, and simmer for 10 minutes, stirring often.

Add the parsley and salt to taste, and serve.

Serves 5 to 8

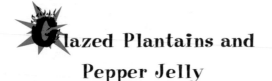

Glazed Plantains and Pepper Jelly

Thanks to Busha Browne for this spicy recipe; all of the ingredients are so reminiscent of Jamaica! Plantains, also called cooking bananas, are popular throughout the Caribbean. These plantains could accompany any meat dish, but we think pork is the best choice.

2 ripe plantains, sliced thin
1/2 cup fresh orange juice
2 tablespoons brown sugar or raw
  cane sugar
2 teaspoons ground allspice,
  Jamaican preferred
2 tablespoons *Busha Browne's Orange*
  ***Pepper Jelly* (or substitute K)**

Preheat the oven to 325 degrees.

Place the plantains in a greased shallow baking pan. Combine all of the remaining ingredients in a bowl, and spread the mixture over the plantains. Bake for 30 to 40 minutes, making sure the plantains do not dry out; add a little more orange juice if necessary.

Serve the plantains hot.

Serves 4

Sedona Red Chilaquiles

According to Goldwater's representatives, this recipe is an easy version of an old Mexican hash recipe. This interesting dish would complement grilled chicken or fish; serve more of Goldwater's Sedona Red Salsa on the side to put on the grilled meat.

1/2 8-ounce bag corn tortilla chips
2 cups sour cream
1 jar *Goldwater's Sedona Red Salsa*
  (or substitute B)
2 cups shredded cheddar cheese

Preheat the oven to 350 degrees.

Layer one-half of the ingredients beginning with the chips and in the order given, in a medium baking dish. Repeat the layering, ending with the cheese. Bake for 30 minutes. Serve the chilaquiles hot.

Variation: Try adding one or more of the following: chicken, chopped onion, jalapeños, or refried beans.

Serves 4 to 6

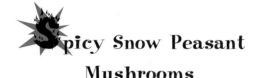

Spicy Snow Peasant Mushrooms

Serve this spicy side dish from Busha Browne to add some pizzazz to your menu. It could also be served over rice or pasta. Use the pepper sherry to liven up other vegetable dishes as well.

1 tablespoon olive oil
1 garlic clove, crushed
2 shallots, chopped
1 cup sliced mushrooms
1 1/2 to 2 cups snow peas
1 1/2 tablespoons *Busha Browne's Spicy and Hot Pepper Sherry* (or substitute P)
1 tablespoon soy sauce (optional)

Heat the olive oil in a skillet and lightly sauté the garlic and shallots. Add the remaining ingredients; continue to sauté, stirring often. Remove the pan from the heat when the vegetables are done but still tender.

Serve the vegetables alone or over rice or pasta.

Serves 4

Sautéed Butternut Squash

Slow cooking brings out the butternut's natural sugars. Fresh sage adds a wonderful contrasting flavor accent. We thank Renee Shepherd of Shepherd's Garden Seeds for this recipe. Her seed catalog contains varieties that are hard to find anywhere else, including some specialty squashes.

3 tablespoons vegetable oil
1 1/2 pounds butternut squash, seeded and cut into 1-inch chunks (about 3 1/2 cups)
1 large garlic clove, minced
Salt and pepper to taste
1 tablespoon chopped sage
1 tablespoon chopped Italian parsley
1 tablespoon minced jalapeño chile

In a heavy skillet (preferable nonstick), heat the oil until it is sizzling. Add the squash and garlic, and toss to coat the squash well with the oil. Sauté the mixture slowly over low heat, stirring frequently, for about 30 minutes, or until the squash is golden and tender (add a tablespoon or two of water if the squash begins to stick). Add salt and pepper, then sprinkle the sage, parsley, and chile over the squash. Mix to combine the ingredients well, and serve.

Serves 4

Princess Street Vegetable Stir-fry

Busha Browne presents this superb vegetable stir-fry. According to Winston Stona, "Princess Street was originally the heart of Kingston's thriving Chinatown and the site of its most famous Chinese restaurant." This dish is best if you include equal amounts of hard and soft vegetables.

2 tablespoons vegetable oil
1-inch piece fresh ginger, peeled and
** crushed (optional)**
2 garlic cloves, peeled and bruised
1/2 teaspoon salt
At least six of the following vegetables:
** 1 large onion, sliced lengthwise and**
** separated; 1/2 cup cauliflower or broccoli**
** florets; 1/2 cup snow peas; 1/2 cup**
** julienned carrots; 1/2 cup fresh sliced**
** mushrooms; 1/2 cup celery cut in 1/2-inch**
** chunks; 1/2 cup cho-cho (chayote squash),**
** thinly sliced; 1/2 cup chopped green**
** onion; 1/2 cup bamboo shoots; 1 cup**
** bean sprouts; 1 cup julienned zucchini;**
** 1 cup coarsely chopped cabbage; 1 cup**
** coarsely chopped bok choy; 1/2 cup sliced**
** water chestnuts**
1 teaspoon soy sauce
1 tablespoon *Busha Browne's Spicy and Hot*
** *Pepper Sherry* (or substitute P)**
1 tablespoon *Busha Browne's Original Spicy*
** *Planter's Sauce* (or substitute D)**

2 tablespoons *Busha Browne's Ginger*
** *Pepper Jelly*, melted in a little water**
** (or substitute K)**
2 tablespoons toasted sunflower seeds

Heat the oil in a wok or skillet. When the oil is hot, add the garlic and ginger, and toss them until their fragrance rises. Remove and discard them.

Add the salt, then the vegetables, one at a time, stirring continually. Start with the hard vegetables; add the leafy vegetables last. When all the vegetables are slightly wilted but still crisp, sprinkle on the soy sauce, the pepper sherry, and the planter's sauce.

Stir in the thinned jelly, and add the sunflower seeds. Cover the wok or skillet, and steam the vegetables for about 5 minutes. Serve the vegetables immediately, straight from the wok or skillet.

Variation: Use cashew nuts instead of water chestnuts.

Serves 6 to 8

outhwest Pinto Beans

Sundance offers this recipe for a bean side dish. Cooking dry beans does take advance preparation (you must soak the beans overnight), but home-cooked beans are superior to the canned variety. Make this recipe on a weekend or when you have enough time, and then freeze the leftovers in packages of 1 to 2 cups each.

2 cups dry pinto or other beans
2 tablespoons canola oil
2 cups chopped onions
1 cup tomato sauce
3 tablespoons *Sundance Southwest Seasoning* (or substitute A)

In a large pot or Dutch oven, soak the beans overnight. Do not drain the beans. Simmer them in their soaking water, covered, for 3 1/2 hours or until they are tender.

Heat a skillet over medium heat, and add the oil. When the oil is hot, add the onion. Sauté until the onion is translucent. Add the sautéed onion, tomato sauce, and Sundance Southwest Seasoning to the beans, and stir well. Simmer the beans uncovered for 30 minutes.

Variation: Substitute 1/2 pound diced bacon for the canola oil. Sauté the bacon with the onion until the bacon is crisp.

Yields 6 cups

egetarian Spectacular

FoFo Voltaire had the first Caribbean food restaurant in Albuquerque, and we were crushed when she closed it to develop her spice products. We may be selfish, but FoFo's food was great! Using her dry spice creations, however, we can re-create those Caribbean flavors she presented at her restaurant.

1 tablespoon olive oil
1 tablespoon diced onion
1 pound fresh vegetables of your choice (try snow peas, broccoli, carrots, and snap beans)
1/4 cup water
1 1/2 tablespoons *FoFo's Vegetarian Spice* (hot or regular) (or substitute A)

Heat the oil in a skillet. Lightly sauté the onion. Add the remaining ingredients, and cover the pan. Steam the vegetables for 4 minutes.

Uncover the pan, and continue cooking, stirring, until the vegetables are tender but still crisp.

Serves 4

Roasted Pepper and Black Bean Salad

This tasty recipe comes from our friends at Shepherd's Garden Seeds, now in their tenth year of business. The catalog grew out of many discussions Renee Shepherd had with a visiting manager of a large European seed company. If you have never tried roasting peppers, do. The peppers take on a new flavor that will add richness to your dishes.

1 1/4 cups dry black beans,
** or 3 cups cooked**
Salt and pepper to taste
2 red bell peppers, halved lengthwise,
** stemmed, and seeded**
2 yellow bell peppers, halved lengthwise,
** stemmed, and seeded**

Dressing:
2 tablespoons fresh lemon juice
1 tablespoon red wine vinegar
1/2 teaspoon ground cumin
1 teaspoon sugar
1 large garlic clove, minced
1/3 cup olive oil
Salt and pepper to taste
1/3 cup chopped fresh basil

2 to 4 scallions, chopped for garnish

If you are using dry beans, bring them to a boil in water to cover by 3 inches. Loosely cover the pot, and simmer the beans for about 1 hour, or until they are tender but not mushy. Season the beans with salt and pepper.

Preheat the oven to 450 degrees. Place the cut peppers on a broiling pan, 3 inches from the heat. Turn the peppers frequently until the skins are blackened, then remove the pan and let the peppers cool. Remove the skins from the peppers, and cut the peppers into 1-inch squares. Combine the peppers with the beans in a large bowl.

Combine the dressing ingredients, and stir them into the bean and pepper mixture. Garnish with the chopped scallions and serve.

Serves 6 to 8

 # Pickled Kohlrabi

These crunchy pickles will call to you every time you open the refrigerator. Renee Shepherd created this recipe for her company, Shepherd's Garden Seeds. If you have never tried kohlrabi, you'll find the texture is like that of a firm apple. Order some seeds from Renee's catalog; she has two varieties.

3 kohlrabi, peeled and sliced 1/4 inch thick
2 large carrots, peeled and cut into sticks,
   and parboiled about 3 minutes
2 garlic cloves, crushed
1 bay leaf
3 large sprigs dill
Pickling Mixture:
3/4 cup white vinegar
1 1/4 cups water
3 tablespoons sugar
1 teaspoon mustard seed
1/2 teaspoon dill seed
1/4 teaspoon dried red pepper flakes
1 teaspoon salt

Mix the kohlrabi and carrots, and pack them in a 1-quart glass jar along with the garlic, bay leaf, and dill.

In a saucepan, combine the pickling mixture. Heat, stirring, until the mixture boils and the sugar dissolves. Pour the boiling mixture over the kohlrabi, filling the jar completely. Place the lid on the jar. Let the jar cool, then refrigerate the pickles for 3 to 4 days to let the flavors blend.

Yields 1 quart

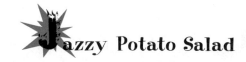 # Jazzy Potato Salad

If you are tired of ordinary potato salads, try this delicious recipe from Sgt. Pepper's, the manufacturer of Jazz! Pepper Vinegar, an integral ingredient in the salad. Serve the potato salad at your next cookout and listen to the raves.

10 medium red potatoes, cut into quarters
1/4 cup cream cheese
1 cup mayonnaise
1/2 cup *Jazz! Pepper Vinegar*
   (or substitute C)
2 hard-boiled eggs
1 jalapeño chile, stemmed, seeded,
   and minced
1 red bell pepper, diced
1 medium white onion, diced
1/2 cup chopped cilantro
Salt to taste

Steam the potatoes until they are tender, approximately 35 minutes. Drain the potatoes, let them cool, and chill them.

To prepare the dressing, combine the cream cheese, mayonnaise, vinegar, eggs, and jalapeño in a blender, and blend until the mixture is smooth.

In a large bowl, combine the potatoes, dressing, red bell pepper, onion, and cilantro. Mix the salad well, season it with salt, and chill it at least 2 hours before serving.

Serves 6 to 8

Asparagus with Roasted Red Peppers and Capers

Our thanks to Mezzetta's for this recipe. This method of cooking asparagus is appealing because the freshness and crunch still remains. The simple, delicious flavors of the red peppers and the capers would complement an entrée of grilled fish.

1 pound fresh asparagus

1 red onion, cut in half, then
  sliced crosswise

3 tablespoons *Mezzetta Extra-Virgin*
  Olive Oil

3/4 cup *Mezzetta Roasted Red Peppers*,
  sliced into strips (or substitute roasted
  red bell peppers)

2 to 3 tablespoons *Mezzetta Imported*
  ***Capers*, drained (or substitute**
  other capers)

1/4 cup lemon juice

1/4 teaspoon habanero hot sauce

Salt and pepper to taste

Blanch the asparagus in boiling water for 2 minutes. Drain the asparagus, and let it cool.

Meanwhile, heat the olive oil in a small skillet. Sauté the onion until it is soft, then add the red peppers and capers. Add the lemon juice, hot sauce, salt, and pepper. Remove the mixture from the heat.

Arrange the asparagus on a platter, and top with the pepper, caper, and onion mixture. Serve at once.

Serves 2 to 4

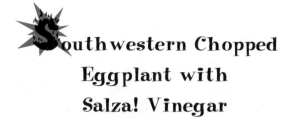

Southwestern Chopped Eggplant with Salza! Vinegar

Many thanks to J. P. Hayes of Sgt. Pepper's, the manufacturer of Texas Tears and Salza! vinegar. Serve this eggplant as a side dish with grilled chicken or pork; it's also good as a spread on crackers.

2 eggplants, thickly sliced crosswise
4 tomatillos, husks removed
2 poblano chiles
1 white onion, diced
2 tablespoons chopped fresh cilantro
1 tablespoon crushed garlic
4 tablespoons canola oil
1/2 teaspoon salt
1/4 teaspoon ground black pepper
2 tablespoons lemon juice
1/2 cup *Salza! Vinegar* (or substitute C)

Preheat the oven to 375 degrees. Place the eggplant, tomatillos, and chiles in a baking pan, and bake them for 35 to 40 minutes. The eggplant may take a little longer.

Remove the outer skin from the eggplant and only the stem from the poblanos, leaving the skin and seeds intact. Coarsely chop the baked ingredients in a food processor; do not puree them.

In a large bowl, combine the remaining ingredients. Add the contents of the food processor to the bowl.

Refrigerate the mixture for 2 hours to allow the flavors to blend, then serve.

Serves 4

arlik Custard

Judy Knapp knows all of the garlic lore: Balkan jockeys rub garlic on the bridles of their horses to make them run faster; Judy feeds her Pikled Garlik to her dog to keep the fleas and ticks away ("My dog loves it," she says). We thank Judy of the Pikled Garlik Company for this great recipe for humans! Serve the custard as a first course or as an accompaniment to roasted meat or fowl.

8 medium cloves **Red Chili Pikled Garlic**
   (or substitute other pickled garlic)
1 cup water
4 egg yolks
2 whole eggs
1 tablespoon salt
2 cups milk
1/8 teaspoon white pepper
Edible flowers or minced parsley,
   for garnish

Preheat the oven to 350 degrees.

In a small saucepan, boil the garlic cloves in 1 cup water for 2 minutes. Remove the garlic, let it cool, and mash it with a fork.

In a bowl, whisk the eggs together, and add the garlic. Stir in the salt, milk, and white pepper. Fill seven 1/4-cup molds or custard cups with the mixture, stirring so that the garlic doesn't settle to the bottom of the bowl. Set the molds in a pan with enough hot water to come about halfway up the sides.

Bake the custard for 30 minutes. Serve it cooled or chilled. Before serving, unmold the custard by running a knife around the edge; turn the custard upside down on the serving plate. Garnish with edible flowers or parsley.

Serves 7

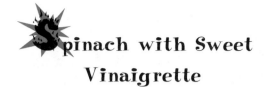 Spinach with Sweet Vinaigrette

Sgt. Pepper's delicious Viva! Italian Vinegar *adds punch to this spinach dish. Sgt. Pepper's believes that a recipe does not have to be long or complicated for the finished dish to taste fantastic, and this dish is evidence of that. The spinach will go well with broiled or grilled meats.*

1 cup olive oil

1/2 cup *Viva! Italian Vinegar*
  (or substitute C)

5 garlic cloves, crushed

2 tablespoons sugar

1/4 teaspoon habanera hot sauce

1 bunch spinach, washed and drained,
  torn into large pieces

1/2 cup lightly toasted pine nuts

1/2 cup crumbled feta cheese

1/2 cup golden raisins

1 red onion, sliced

In a blender, combine the oil, vinegar, garlic, sugar, and hot sauce. Refrigerate the dressing for 2 hours. Mix it well before using it.

In a serving bowl, combine the spinach, pine nuts, feta cheese, raisins, and red onion. Toss the contents with the dressing, and serve.

Serves 4

Brave Breads
and Dazzling Desserts

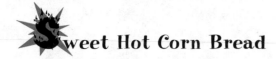

Sweet Hot Corn Bread

This sweet and spicy corn bread will be great with your favorite barbecue dish. We thank John and Diane Cannon of Cannon Unlimited for the recipe, which incorporates one of their delicious products, Cannon's Sweet Hot Peppers.

3/4 cup sifted all-purpose flour
2 1/2 teaspoons double-acting
   baking powder
1 to 2 tablespoons sugar
3/4 teaspoon salt
1 1/4 cups yellow or white cornmeal
1 egg
2 to 3 tablespoons melted butter
   or meat drippings
1 cup milk
1/4 cup chopped *Cannon's Sweet Hot
   Peppers* (or substitute 1 tablespoon
   chopped jalapeño, 3 tablespoons chopped
   bell pepper, and 1 teaspoon sugar)

Preheat the oven to 425 degrees. Grease or butter a baking pan or skillet, and place it in the hot oven.

Sift together the dry ingredients. In another bowl, combine the butter or drippings, egg, and milk, and pour the liquid into the dry mixture. Fold in the peppers, and pour the batter into the hot pan. Bake for 25 minutes.

Serve the corn bread hot.

Serves 6 to 8

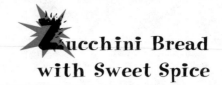

Zucchini Bread with Sweet Spice

Do you always end up with too much zucchini from your garden? Greg Deneen from Santa Fe Seasons offers this delicious zucchini bread recipe, which uses one of his fine products. We like the bread warm with a little cream cheese spread on it.

3 eggs
2 cups sugar
1 cup vegetable oil
2 cups puréed zucchini (leave the skins on)
1 teaspoon vanilla extract
1/2 teaspoon baking powder
1 1/2 teaspoons baking soda
3 teaspoons *Santa Fe Seasons Sweet Spices*
   (or substitute A)
3 cups sifted flour
1 teaspoon salt
3/4 cup walnut or pecan meats

Preheat the oven to 350 degrees. Grease and flour two loaf pans.

In a large bowl, beat together the eggs and sugar until the mixture is fluffy. Stir in the remaining ingredients. Pour the mixture into the bread pans, and bake the loaves for 50 to 60 minutes, until they test done.

Yields 2 loaves

Spicy Cheese Bread

Thanks to Lora Brody, Barbara Hunter, and the McIlhenny Company for this hot and spicy bread recipe. We think this bread would make an ordinary sandwich sizzle!

2 envelopes active dry yeast

1 teaspoon sugar

1/2 cup warm water (110 degrees)

8 1/2 cups all-purpose flour

3 cups shredded Jarlsberg or Swiss cheese

2 tablespoons chopped rosemary,
  or 2 teaspoons dried

1 tablespoon salt

1 tablespoon *Tabasco Pepper Sauce*
  (or substitute D)

2 cups milk

4 large eggs

In a small bowl, stir together the yeast, sugar, and warm water. Let the mixture stand for 5 minutes or until it is foamy.

Meanwhile, in a large bowl combine 8 cups of the flour, the cheese, the rosemary, the salt, and the Tabasco.

In a small saucepan over low heat, heat the milk until it is warm (120 to 130 degrees). Stir the milk into the flour mixture. In a medium bowl, lightly beat the eggs. Remove 1 tablespoon of the egg to brush onto the dough later. Add the remaining eggs to the flour mixture along with the foamy yeast mixture. Stir to make a soft dough.

On a lightly floured surface, knead the dough, incorporating the remaining 1/2 cup flour, for 5 minutes or until the dough becomes smooth and elastic. Shape the dough into a ball, and place it in a large greased bowl, turning the dough over to grease its entire surface. Cover the bowl with a towel, and let the dough rise in a warm place until it has doubled in size (about 1 1/2 hours). Grease two large cookie sheets. Punch down the dough and cut it in half. Cut each half into thirds; roll each piece into a rope, and braid each trio of ropes together. Place both braids on the cookie sheet. Cover them, and let them rise in a warm place until they are almost doubled (30 minutes to 1 hour).

Preheat the oven to 375 degrees. Brush the braids with the reserved egg. Bake them about 45 minutes, or until the braids sound hollow when they are lightly tapped. Remove the bread to wire racks to cool.

Yields 2 loaves

Blue Cornmeal Green Chile Fritters

Chef W. C. Longacre, now of W. C.'s Mountain Road Café in Albuquerque, calls his cuisine "New Hong Key," a tongue-in-cheek reference to his cooking stints in New Mexico, Hong Kong, and Key West. These fritters are good as a side dish, a snack, or even an unusual dessert.

I cup finely ground blue cornmeal
1/2 cup white cornmeal
1/2 cup all-purpose flour
1/4 cup sugar
1/2 teaspoon baking powder
1/4 teaspoon baking soda
I teaspoon salt
I teaspoon ground white pepper
1/3 cup finely chopped New Mexican green
  chile, thoroughly patted dry
1/4 cup finely chopped red bell pepper
1/3 cup milk
1/3 cup beer (preferably Dos Equis)
I whole egg plus I egg yolk, lightly beaten
2 1/2 tablespoons corn oil
I teaspoon vanilla extract
Vegetable oil, for frying

In a large bowl, mix the cornmeals, flour, sugar, baking powder, baking soda, salt, and white pepper. Stir in the green chile and red bell pepper. Lightly mix in the milk, beer, eggs, oil, and vanilla. If the mixture seems too dry, add a little more milk. Using a 3/4-ounce scoop or your hands, fashion the batter into about 24 fritters.

Heat the vegetable oil in a deep-fryer or deep skillet. Add the fritters, a few at a time, and fry them until they are evenly browned. Drain them on paper towels and keep them warm until all are done.

To serve the fritters as a dessert, provide chocolate syrup, maple syrup, or your favorite preserves for dipping. Try mixing cream cheese, orange marmalade, and cinnamon together for an unusual dip.

Yields about 24 fritters

very Island Pirogues

A pirogue is a sturdy, flat-bottom skiff that Louisiana fishermen use to gather the bounty of the bayou, notably the succulent crawfish. These boats, so much a part of life on Avery Island, home of Tabasco Pepper Sauce, inspired the name and shape of these rolls, which get their zing and zest from Tabasco. Try using an Avery Island pirogue to scoop up a mess of boiled crawfish. We thank Lora Brody, Barbara Hunter, and the McIlhenny Company for this bread machine recipe.

1 tablespoon yeast

3 cups bread flour

1/3 cup yellow cornmeal

1/3 cup chile oil

1 extra large egg

1/2 cup chopped onion

1/4 cup minced cilantro

1 cup water (reserve 1/4 to add
   after kneading)

1 teaspoon salt

1 teaspoon *Tabasco Crushed Pepper*
   (or substitute any crushed red chile)

1/4 teaspoon *Tabasco Pepper Sauce* or
   1 teaspoon Tabasco Jalapeño Sauce
   (or substitute D)

Put all of the ingredients in the order listed, in a bread machine. Program the machine for manual, and press start. At the end of the final kneading cycle, remove the dough to a lightly floured work space.

Divide the dough into two pieces, and roll each piece into an 8-inch rope. Cut each rope into four pieces. Roll each piece into a 5-inch "cigar," and place the cigars 2 inches apart on a baking sheet dusted with cornmeal. Use your fingers to gently flatten each cigar, applying the most pressure in the middle and tapering the ends so that you have a long oval.

Cover the pirogues with a clean dish towel, and allow them to rise for 30 minutes, or until they are doubled in bulk.

To bake:

1 tablespoon olive oil

2 tablespoons coarse jalapeño salt or
   Tabasco All-Purpose Seasoned Salt
   (or substitute any seasoning salt)

Preheat the oven to 450 degrees and set the rack in the center position. Brush the top of each pirogue with olive oil, and sprinkle the pirogue with the seasoned salt. Bake the pirogues for 15 to 17 minutes, or until their tops turn golden brown. Serve them warm.

Serves 6 to 8

hili Chingaso Bread

Andy Housholder of HI-CO Western Products qualifies as one of the people having the most ingredients in a recipe in this cookbook! This recipe makes a large quantity of rich cornbread.

2 cups (16 ounces) corn muffin mix

2 cups masa harina

1 3/4 cups cream-style corn

1 3/4 cups whole kernel corn
 (drained if canned)

2 cups roasted, peeled, seeded, and diced
 green chile

1/2 cup roasted, peeled, seeded, and diced
 jalapeño peppers

1 large onion, in 1/4-inch dice

1 cup bottled salsa

1/2 cup finely chopped green onion
 or chives

4 extra large eggs

6 slices cooked bacon, crumbled

2 ounces cream cheese

1 teaspoon salt

1 tablespoon dark brown sugar

1/4 cup corn oil

2 tablespoons *Fiesta Shake*

1 teaspoon *Green Jalapeño Chili Powder*
 (or substitute any red chile powder)

2 tablespoons *Mild Green Chili Powder*
 (or substitute any green or red pure chile
 powder)

1 teaspoon minced cilantro

1 1/2 cups mild cheddar cheese, cut into
 1/4 inch cubes

Milk

Preheat the oven to 350 degrees.

In a large mixing bowl, combine all of the ingredients except the milk and cheddar cheese. Stir in enough milk to the desired thickness, and then add the cheddar cheese cubes.

Pour the mixture into two buttered ovenproof glass 8-inch-square baking dishes.

Bake the bread for 15 minutes, then reduce the heat to 325 degrees, and bake approximately 30 minutes more, until the bread tests done. Turn off the oven, and leave the bread in the oven for about 15 minutes more.

Remove the pan to a rack, and let it cool before cutting it.

(With some electric ovens, it may be necessary to bake the bread on the top rack and insert on the lower rack a heavy-duty roasting pan, to help keep the bottom of the bread from burning due to the long exposure to the infrared heat of the cooking element.)

Yields 2 8-inch-square dishes of cornbread

Serves 10 to 12

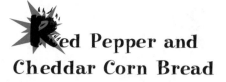

Red Pepper and Cheddar Corn Bread

Thanks to G. L. Mezzetta for this quick recipe, which makes a tasty accompaniment to bowls of red chili. Try this cornbread at the next cookout instead of yeast bread or rolls.

8 1/2 ounces corn muffin mix
7 1/2 ounces *Mezzetta Roasted Red Peppers*, drained and chopped
1/2 cup shredded cheddar cheese
Pinch ground dried red pepper, or more, to taste

Preheat the oven to 400 degrees. Grease an 8-inch-square baking dish.

Prepare the batter according to the corn muffin package directions. Stir in the chopped red peppers, cheese, and ground red pepper. Spread the mixture evenly in the prepared pan, and bake 27 minutes, or until the bread tests done.

Remove the pan to a rack, and let it cool for 10 minutes.

Cut the cornbread into 16 2-inch squares while it is still in the pan, and serve it warm.

Serves 4 to 6

iñata Bread

Old El Paso Foods gave us this terrific recipe for fast and spicy bread. Serve it for brunch, with eggs (and more picante sauce, heated), and, of course, hash-browns (with picante sauce added as they cook). Or serve the bread with hot and spicy grilled meat at your next cookout.

12 ounces (10 count) refrigerator biscuits
1 cup *Old El Paso Thick 'n' Chunky Picante Salsa*
1 cup shredded jack cheese
***Old El Paso Pickled Jalapeño Slices* (or substitute B) (or substitute other pickled jalapeños)**

Preheat the oven to 375 degrees. Cut each biscuit into quarters. In a bowl, combine the biscuit pieces and 1/2 cup of the salsa, and stir to coat the biscuit pieces evenly. Put the biscuit pieces into a greased 9-inch pie pan, and arrange them in a single layer.

In a small bowl, combine the remaining 1/2 cup salsa and the cheese. Spoon this mixture over the biscuits, and garnish with the jalapeño slices.

Bake the bread for 30 to 35 minutes or until the center is completely cooked.

Serves 5

Bitchy Bread

How about some hot and spicy sausage or some spicy barbecued meat between two pieces of this hot and spicy bread? It gives new meaning to having a hot lunch date. Chip Hearn of Peppers, and owner of the Starboard Restaurant, probably thought of this too, when he created this recipe.

1 6-ounce frozen loaf white bread dough, thawed and cubed
1 tablespoon minced red bell pepper
1 tablespoon minced yellow bell pepper
1 tablespoon minced onion
1 tablespoon shredded cheddar cheese
1 tablespoon *Chunky Style Delaware Destroyer* (or substitute B)
1 teaspoon *Hot Bitch at the Beach*

Mix all of the ingredients in a bowl. Put the mixture into a loaf pan, and set the pan in a warm place until the dough doubles in size.

Preheat the oven to 350 degrees. Bake the bread for 20 minutes.

Remove the bread from the oven, slice it, and serve it with chunky *Delaware Destroyer* or your favorite barbecue or honey mustard sauce.

Serves 4 to 6

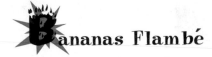

Bananas Flambé

We thank Stacy Tanner of Bowman's Landing Epicurean Company for this elegant, tasty recipe. There is nothing quite as impressive as serving a flaming dessert to really impress your guests!

4 bananas, split lengthwise
1/4 cup butter
1/4 cup lime juice
1/4 cup sugar
Ground cinnamon to taste
Ground nutmeg to taste
1/4 cup light or dark rum

Preheat the oven to 350 degrees.

Place the bananas in a buttered shallow baking dish. Mix together the lime juice and sugar, and pour the mixture over the bananas. Sprinkle the bananas with the cinnamon and nutmeg. Bake the bananas for 20 minutes. Remove the dish from the oven.

Heat the rum, and pour it over the cooked bananas. Ignite the rum, and serve the dessert when the flame dies. Accompany the bananas with whipped cream or ice cream.

Serves 4

pple Tart in Pistachio Pastry

As we were typing this recipe, all we could think of was an imaginary letter: "Dear Marianne Schweers: Would you please make this pastry immediately and bring it to us? We are addicted to The Heart of the Desert Pistachios and would like some relief with this delicious recipe." Need we say more?

1 1/2 cups all-purpose flour

6 tablespoons sugar

3/4 cup butter or margarine, cut into small pieces

1/2 cup finely chopped *Heart of the Desert Pistachios* (or substitute E)

1 1/2 pounds baking apples, cored and sliced into thin rings

3/4 cup apple jelly, currant jelly, or apricot jam

Preheat the oven to 450 degrees.

To make the pastry, combine the flour and 4 tablespoons of the sugar. Blend the flour mixture with the butter until it is crumbly yet moist (it should clump between your fingertips). Mix in 1/4 cup pistachios, and press the mixture gently onto the bottom and sides of a 9-inch tart pan with a removable bottom. Bake the pastry for 13 to 15 minutes, or until it is light golden brown in the center.

Remove the pastry from the oven, and let it cool.

To make the filling, combine the apple slices and the remaining 2 tablespoons sugar in a skillet. Cover the skillet, and cook the apples over medium heat, stirring twice, for 13 to 15 minutes, or until the apples are tender but not limp. Drain the apples and let them cool.

To assemble the tart, overlap the apple slices in the pastry shell in a spiral pattern, starting at the edge and working inward. Beat the jelly with a spoon until it is smooth (if you are using apricot jam, force the jam through a sieve, then beat it). Spoon the jelly or jam evenly over the apples. Sprinkle the remaining 1/4 cup pistachios in a ring around the edge of the tart. Remove the tart from the pan before serving.

Serves 6 to 8

Rum Sauce

For those of you who have a sweet tooth and like rum, this recipe from Chef Landry, owner of Byron's Catering, should satisfy you. Serve the sauce over a slice of mincemeat pie, raisin pie, or bread pudding.

2 quarts cold water

3 cups sugar

3/4 teaspoon salt

5 tablespoons butter or margarine

1/2 cup all-purpose flour

1/2 teaspoon ground mace

3/4 teaspoon ground cinnamon

1/4 cup rum

In a saucepan, bring the water, 1 1/2 cups sugar, and the salt to a boil.

In another saucepan, melt the butter. Add the flour, and cook, stirring constantly, over high heat for 2 minutes. Add the remaining sugar, the mace, the cinnamon, and the rum. Beat the liquid into the butter-flour mixture. Beat until all of the ingredients are mixed well.

Serve the rum sauce hot.

Yields 2 quarts

Heart of the Desert Ten-Minute Pistachio Brittle

When you suddenly get a craving for something sweet, try this fast and easy recipe from Marianne Schweers of the Heart of the Desert Pistachio Company. It will satisfy even the most jaded of palates.

1 cup sugar

1/2 cup light corn syrup

1/8 teaspoon salt

1 to 1 1/2 cups *Heart of the Desert* pistachio nutmeats (or substitute E)

1 tablespoon butter

1 teaspoon vanilla extract

1 teaspoon baking soda

Combine the sugar, syrup, and salt in a 2-quart casserole or mixing bowl. Microwave the mixture on high heat for 5 minutes. Stir in the pistachios. Microwave again for 2 to 5 minutes, stirring after 2 and 4 minutes, until the syrup and pistachios are lightly browned. Stir in the butter, vanilla, and baking soda. Stir until the mixture is light and foamy.

Spread the mixture to a 1/4 inch thickness on a large, well-buttered cookie sheet. For very thin pistachio brittle, lift the brittle from the sheet after 3 to 5 minutes, and stretch the candy to the desired thickness.

Yields 2 cups

Busha's Banana Fritters

Thanks to Busha Browne for this tropical dessert recipe. Be sure to serve these fritters with the marmalade sauce for some extra zip.

Marmalade Sauce:
1/2 cup *Busha Browne's Burned Orange Marmalade* **(or substitute other marmalade)**
1/2 cup boiling water
1 tablespoon cornstarch
2 tablespoons cold water
1/4 cup brandy or aged Jamaican gold rum
Fritters:
3 tablespoons all-purpose flour
1/2 teaspoon baking powder
3 ripe bananas
1 teaspoon lime juice
1 whole egg
1 tablespoon sugar
2 tablespoons vegetable oil

In a small saucepan, melt the marmalade in the boiling water. Dissolve the cornstarch in the cold water and add it to the hot mixture. Heat to thicken the mixture. Then stir in the brandy or rum, and mix thoroughly. Remove the sauce from the heat. Keep it warm while you make the fritters.

Sift together the flour and baking powder.

In another bowl, quickly mash the bananas until they are smooth, and then stir in the lime juice.

In a separate bowl, beat the egg and sugar together. Stir in the bananas and the flour mixture.

Pour the oil into a skillet over medium heat. When the skillet is hot, drop in the batter by spoonfuls, and fry the fritters until they are crisp.

Serve the fritters hot, drizzled with the marmalade sauce. Serves 3

Asian-style Poached Pears with Serrano Chile Honey Sauce

W. C. Longacre, who has performed cooking demonstrations at the Fiery Foods Show for years, has come up with a stunning hot and spicy dessert that's certain to please the most dedicated chilehead.

4 firm Bosc pears, peeled, halved, and seeded

2 quarts cool water

2 teaspoons salt

Juice of 1 lemon

6 whole cloves

4 whole star anise

2 tablespoons grated fresh ginger

1 cup Gewürztraminer wine

1 1/2 tablespoons vanilla extract

1/4 cup grenadine syrup

2 1/2 cups sugar

2 serrano chiles, stemmed, seeded, and minced

1/2 cup honey (orange blossom is especially good)

2 tablespoons dark rum

2 ounces shaved dark chocolate

Strawberries or orange slices, for garnish

In a large bowl, combine the pears, water, 1 teaspoon salt, and the lemon juice and allow the pears to marinate.

In a 4-quart saucepan, combine the cloves, anise, ginger, wine, vanilla, grenadine, and 2 cups sugar, and bring the mixture to a boil, stirring constantly. When the sugar is dissolved, drain the pears, and carefully add them to the saucepan. Add enough water to just cover the pears, and reduce the heat. Simmer the pears until they look translucent; do not overcook them.

Remove the pears from the poaching liquid, place them on a cookie sheet, and place the sheet in the freezer for 20 to 25 minutes. Then remove the pears to the refrigerator, and cover them loosely with plastic wrap.

Briskly boil the poaching liquid in a saucepan until it is reduced to 2 cups. Add the chiles, 1/2 cup sugar, and the honey, and bring the sauce to a slow boil. Reduce the heat, and simmer for 2 minutes. Turn off the heat, stir in the rum, and let the sauce cool slightly.

To serve, set two pear halves on each chilled dessert plate, ladle some of the sauce over the pears, top with a portion of chocolate, and add the garnish.

Serves 4

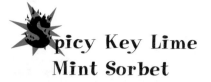

Spicy Key Lime Mint Sorbet

This sorbet will stimulate the palate with the heat of the habanero. If you don't have any key limes, fresh Persian limes will work equally well, but don't substitute dried mint for the fresh. Many thanks to Los Dos for this recipe.

1 1/4 cups sugar
1 cup water
1/3 cup firmly packed mint leaves
1/4 teaspoon *Los Dos Gourmet Habanero Chile Powder* (or substitute other chile powder)
3 cups fresh lime juice (from about 16 limes)
2 tablespoons gin (optional)

Combine the sugar with the water in a saucepan, and bring the mixture to a boil. Boil, stirring, until all the sugar has dissolved. Remove the syrup from the heat, and let it cool.

Combine the syrup and mint in a blender or food processor, and purée until the mixture is smooth. Stir in the chile powder, the lime juice, and, if you like, the gin, and refrigerate the mixture for an hour.

Freeze the mixture in an ice cream machine, following the manufacturer's directions.

Yields 1 quart

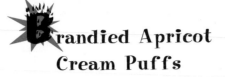

Brandied Apricot Cream Puffs

This light, flavorful, elegant dessert is a guaranteed hit. We thank Cynthia and Jim Fowler of Southwest Spirit for the recipe, which uses one of their fine products. The Brandied Apricots Diablo are "Tangy, blessed with brandy, and sparkling with chile."

Pastry:
1/2 cup margarine or butter
1 cup boiling water
1 cup flour
1/4 teaspoon salt
4 eggs
Filling:
2/3 cup sugar
2 tablespoons all-purpose flour
2 tablespoons cornstarch
1/2 teaspoon salt
3 cups milk
2 slightly beaten egg yolks
2 teaspoons brandy
Southwest Spirit Brandied Apricots Diablo
   (or substitute K)
Chocolate sauce

Preheat the oven to 450 degrees.

In a saucepan, melt the margarine in the boiling water. Add the flour and salt, and stir vigorously. Cook, stirring constantly, until the mixture forms a ball. Remove the pan from the heat. Add the eggs one at a time, and beat until the mixture is smooth.

Drop the dough by heaping tablespoons at least 3 inches apart on a greased cookie sheet. Bake the cream puff shells for 15 minutes, then reduce the heat to 325 degrees. Bake for 25 minutes more. Remove the puffs from the oven, and turn off the heat. Split the shells in half with a knife, and return them to the oven open-faced for another 30 minutes.

In the meantime, make the filling: In a saucepan, mix the sugar, flour, cornstarch, and salt. Gradually stir in the milk. Cook, stirring until the mixture thickens and boils; then cook and stir for 2 minutes longer. Stir a little of the hot mixture into the egg yolks, and then stir the egg yolks into the hot mixture. Stirring constantly, bring the mixture almost to a boil. Add the brandy. Remove the pan from the heat, and beat until the filling is smooth.

Fill the bottom half of each cream puff shell with the custard filling. Pour approximately 1/4 cup Southwest Spirit Brandied Apricots Diablo over the filling, and cover with the top half of the pastry. Spoon chocolate sauce over the top, and serve.

Serves 4 to 6

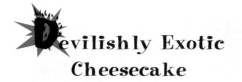Devilishly Exotic Cheesecake

Southwest Spirit's Brandied Cherries Diablo is a mild salsa, full of cherries, and with a hint of brandy and other ingredients that combine to make an ordinary occasion devilishly exotic. Many thanks to Southwest Spirit for this recipe.

2 pounds cream cheese
1 1/3 cups sugar
4 eggs
2 cups sour cream
2 teaspoons brandy
1/3 cup *Southwest Spirit Brandied*
  ***Cherries Diablo* (or substitute K)**

Preheat the oven to 275 degrees.

In a large bowl, beat the cream cheese with the sugar until the mixture is smooth. Add the eggs one at a time, beating thoroughly after each addition, then stir in the sour cream and brandy. Spoon half the cheesecake mixture into a springform pan. Drop the Southwest Spirit Brandied Cherries Diablo by spoonfuls over the cheesecake mixture, and top with the rest of the batter. With a dull knife, lightly swirl the mixture a couple of times. Place the pan on a cookie sheet, and bake for 1 hour.

Remove the baked cheesecake from the oven, and let it cool. Refrigerate it overnight. Unmold the cheesecake and serve it.

Serves 8 to 10

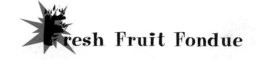Fresh Fruit Fondue

Since 1982, Mick's Peppourri has been producing wonderful products. The company's fine products enhance the flavor of many foods.

This recipe from Mick's is very simple, yet very good.

1/2 cup *Mick's Pepper Jelly*
  (or substitute K)
1/2 cup cream cheese or lemon yogurt
Seasonal fresh fruits

Combine the jelly and cream cheese or yogurt, and let the mixture set in the refrigerator for approximately 1 hour so the flavors will marry.

Serve the mixture as a dip with fresh fruits.

Serves 4

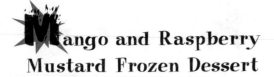 ango and Raspberry
Mustard Frozen Dessert

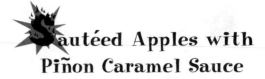 autéed Apples with
Piñon Caramel Sauce

This easy, tangy, refreshing dessert can be stored in the freezer for a few days which makes it the perfect dessert for a party. Thanks to Norman Bishop Mustards for this unusual recipe.

Santa Fe Seasons has created this luscious recipe using one of the company's many fine products. For the freshest flavor, make this dessert when apples are in season.

3 large or 6 medium mangos
3 tablespoons powdered sugar
1/4 cup plain yogurt
1 teaspoon *Norman Bishop Raspberry Mustard* (or substitute H)
Chopped mint or whole raspberries, for garnish

1 tablespoon butter
2 apples, peeled and sliced
3/4 cup *Santa Fe Seasons Pinon Caramel Sauce* (or substitute other caramel sauce)
1/4 cup heavy cream or half-and-half

Peel the mangos, put them in a food processor or blender, and purée them. Add the powdered sugar, and purée again. Blend in the yogurt and mustard into the mangos. Pour the mixture into molds and freeze overnight or longer.

Melt the butter in a large skillet, and add the apple slices. Sauté the apples over medium heat for 1 minute. Then add the caramel sauce, and continue cooking, stirring frequently, until the apples are soft and brown and the sauce is caramelized.

Unmold the dessert about 5 minutes before serving. Garnish with chopped mint or fresh raspberries. Serve the dessert with thin wafer cookies.

Remove the skillet from the heat. Stir in the cream, scraping the caramel from the bottom of the pan. Divide the dessert among bowls, and serve it warm.

Serves 4 to 6

Serves 4

New Mexico Biscochito Shortbread

This shortbread, flavored with lard, freezes well, and it is the easiest biscochito west of the Rockies to make. We thank the people who created the Southwest Seasons Cookbook for this recipe. Proceeds from the cookbook sales benefit Casa Angelica for Children.

1 cup lard
2 cups all-purpose flour
1/2 cup powdered sugar
2 teaspoons anise seed
1/3 cup sugar
1 teaspoon ground cinnamon

Preheat the oven to 350 degrees.

Blend the flour, powdered sugar, and anise into the lard just until the dough is mixed. Pat the dough into an ungreased 9-inch-square baking pan. Pierce the dough with a fork every 1/2 inch. Mix the sugar and cinnamon, and sprinkle it on the dough. Bake the shortbread for 25 minutes.

Cut the shortbread into bars while it is still warm.

Serves 12

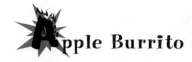
Apple Burrito

This dessert recipe from Leona's Foods of Chimayo, New Mexico, is fast, easy, and delicious. Their tortillas are great, and so are the company's other products.

1 apple, sliced paper-thin
Cinnamon to taste
Sugar to taste
2 *Leona's De Chimayo Flavored Tortillas* (no substitute)
Ice cream or heavy cream, for garnish

Mix the apple slices with the cinnamon and sugar. Spread the apples on the flavored tortillas. Roll up each tortilla burrito-style. Heat the burritos in a microwave oven.

Top the apple burritos with ice cream or whipped cream.

Serves 2

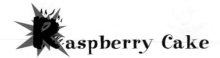

Raspberry Cake

Because this delicious cake is so rich, we suggest serving it after a light entrée. The cake freezes well. We thank all the people who created the Southwest Seasons Cookbook *for this recipe.*

Crust:
1 1/2 cups all-purpose flour
1/2 cup sugar
1 teaspoon baking powder
1/2 cup unsalted butter
1 egg
1/2 cup good-quality raspberry jam
Filling:
1/2 cup butter
2/3 cup sugar
1/2 teaspoon almond extract
2 eggs
1 cup ground almonds
Frosting:
1/2 cup powdered sugar
2 teaspoons fresh lemon juice

Preheat the oven to 350 degrees.

Grease a 9-inch springform pan. Make the crust: In a bowl, blend the flour, sugar, and baking powder together. Blend in the butter, and mix in the egg. Press the dough evenly on the bottom of the pan. Spread 1/4 cup of the raspberry jam over the bottom of the dough. Cover the pan, and chill the dough for 5 minutes while you make the filling.

In a bowl, cream the butter, sugar, and almond extract. Add the eggs, and beat well. Stir the ground almonds into the mixture. Spoon the filling on top of the chilled crust. Bake the cake for 50 minutes.

Remove the cake from the oven, and let it cool in the pan. Then remove the cake carefully from the pan. Spread the remaining raspberry jam over the top.

To make the frosting, mix the powdered sugar and the lemon juice together, and drizzle the mixture over the jam.

Yields 8 servings

Capirotada

This recipe, a sweet treat from the Southwest Seasons Cookbook, *was created by the Santa Fe School of Cooking.* Capirotada *is the Southwest version of bread pudding, and it is so good that we could make a meal of it. The recipe can be doubled or halved.*

12 to 14 slices day-old French bread
1/2 cup pine nuts or pecans
2 cups sugar
3 1/3 cups water
1/2 cup raisins
1 teaspoon ground cinnamon
5 tablespoons unsalted butter
1 1/2 teaspoons vanilla extract
1 cup shredded jack or longhorn cheese
Whipped cream, for garnish

Preheat the oven to 350 degrees.

Tear the bread into 1-inch pieces and toast the pieces on a cookie sheet in the oven for 10 minutes. Then place the toasted bread in a large mixing bowl, and add the nuts.

Put the sugar into a heavy saucepan over a medium heat. Stir continuously with a wire whisk until the sugar melts and turns a caramel color. Immediately add the water, but be very careful, because the syrup will bubble and splatter. The syrup may partially solidify, but if it does, it will liquefy again as it reheats. Reduce the heat, and add the cinnamon, raisins, butter, and vanilla to the syrup while it is still hot. Continue to heat and stir the mixture until the butter has melted.

Pour the syrup over the bread pieces, and toss them lightly. Place this mixture in a buttered ovenproof dish, about 8 by 11 inches. Top the bread with the cheese and bake for 30 minutes.

Serve the *capirotada* warm with the whipped cream.

Yields 6 to 8 servings

Banana Jama Bran Muffins

The habanero heat from the sauce adds a little "kick" to these moist muffins. They are great for breakfast, snacks or even as a dessert as they are not as heavy as the usual bran muffin. Thanks to Los Dos for this terrific recipe.

1 cup all-purpose flour
1 1/2 teaspoons baking soda
3/4 teaspoon salt
1 1/2 cups wheat bran
1 cup chopped walnuts
3/4 cup butter or margarine
2/3 cup sugar
2 cups mashed ripe bananas
1/4 cup *Banana Jama Sauce*
   (or substitute J)
3 eggs, at room temperature

Preheat the oven to 375 degrees.

Grease tins for 24 muffins. Sift the flour, baking soda, and salt together. Mix in the bran and nuts.

In another bowl, cream the margarine. Add the sugar a little at a time, beating well after each addition. Mix in the bananas, the sauce, and, one at a time, the eggs. Stir the banana mixture into the flour mixture; mix only until the dry ingredients are moistened. Pour the batter into the muffin tins, and bake for 15 minutes, or until the muffins are golden brown.

Allow the muffins to cool before removing them from the tins.

Yields 24

Lemon Bars

Many thanks to Chef Scott Landry, owner of Byron's Catering, for this recipe. Lemon bars are easier to make than individual cookies, and they taste great.

4 cups cake flour
4 cups sugar
2 cups unsalted butter, softened
8 large eggs
4 cups powdered sugar
1/2 cup all-purpose flour
1 teaspoon baking powder
1 cup lemon juice

Preheat the oven to 350 degrees.

In a bowl, combine the flour, sugar, and butter, and mix until the dough is well blended. Spread the dough on a cookie sheet, and bake until the crust is lightly browned, about 8 to 10 minutes. Remove the cookie sheet, but leave the oven on.

Beat together the eggs, sugar, flour, baking powder, and lemon juice until the mixture is smooth. Pour this mixture over the crust, and bake for 25 minutes.

Let cool before cutting. Cut into 2" squares.

Yields 2 to 4 dozen

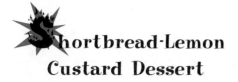

Shortbread-Lemon Custard Dessert

This rich and lemony dessert is definitely for those who love sweets! We thank Scot Robinson of The Santa Fe Cookie Company.

1 1/2 cups **Santa Fe Cookie Company Shortbread Cookies, crushed**
   (or substitute other shortbread cookies)
6 to 8 tablespoons melted butter
   or margarine
2 tablespoons half-and-half
8 egg yolks
1 cup sugar
6 tablespoons fresh lemon juice
4 teaspoons grated lemon rind

Preheat the oven to 300 degrees.

Mix together the crushed cookies, butter or margarine, and half-and-half in a medium bowl. Spread the mixture in an 8-inch-square glass baking dish. Press the mixture firmly on the bottom and about 1/2 inch up the sides of the dish. Bake the crust 10 to 15 minutes; check every few minutes to make sure it isn't getting too brown.

Remove the pan from the oven, and let the crust cool before adding the filling.

In a bowl, beat the egg yolks until they are thick and lemon-colored. Gradually beat in the sugar, and then beat in the juice and the rind.

Transfer the mixture to the top of a double boiler, and cook it over hot water, stirring constantly, until the mixture is thick, about 5 to 8 minutes. Remove the custard from the heat, and let it cool.

When the mixture has cooled, pour it into the cooled shortbread crust. Refrigerate the dessert for several hours before serving.

Serves 6

Resources

Fiery Food Festivals

This list features a number of fiery foods shows held throughout the United States. We have listed the 1995 show dates. You should call the shows directly for information on future show dates.

**Miller Genuine Draft
Hot & Spicy Food Festival**
Naval Air Station
Marietta, GA
(404) 872-4731
May 20

**New England
Hot & Spicy Food Festival**
Hynes Convention Center
Boston, MA
(617) 928-1084
June 17
(call for exact date, subject to change)

**Austin Chronicle
Hot Sauce Contest**
Travis County Farmers Market
Austin, TX
(512) 454-5766
August 26-27

Hatch Chile Festival
Fairgrounds
Hatch, NM
(505) 267-4847
September 2-3

Northwest Fiery Foods Festival
Pasco, WA
(509) 373-5094
September 9-10

Santa Fe Wine and Chile Festival
Downtown
Santa Fe, NM
(505) 983-7929
September 28-Oct. 1

**ICS World's Championship
Chili Cookoff**
Reno, NV
(714) 631-1780
September 29 - Oct. 1

Chile Pepper Fiesta
Brooklyn Botanic Garden
Brooklyn NY
(718) 622-1780
October 1

**The Great Miller Lite
Chili Cookoff**
Stone Mountain Park, GA
404-872-4731
October 14

La Fiesta de los Chiles
Tucson Botanical Gardens,
Tucson, AZ
602-326-9686
October 21-22

**CASI Terlingua
Chili Championship**
Terlingua, TX
817-365-2504
November 5

**The Original Viva Terlingua
International Frank X. Tolbert-
Wick Fowler Memorial
Championship Chili Cookoff**
Arturo White's Store
Terlingua TX
Al Hopkins
(903) 874-5601
November 5

AND

Mark your
calendar for

The 8th Annual National Fiery Foods Show

March 1-3, 1996

**Albuquerque
Convention Center**

Albuquerque, NM

**Call Sunbelt Shows
(505) 873-9103**

Further Reading

Below is a listing of our favorite books concerning either hot and spicy cooking or cuisines that use chile peppers. The books are available from booksellers or libraries.

Andrews, Jean
1984. *Peppers: The Domesticated Capsicums.* Austin: University of Texas Press.
1993. *Red Hot Peppers.* New York: Macmillan.

Bosland, Paul W.
1992. *Capsicum: A Comprehensive Bibliography.* Las Cruces, NM: Chile Institute.

Bridges, Bill
1994. *The Great American Chili Book.* New York: Lyons and Burford

Brown, Bob, et al.
1971. *South American Cookbook.* New York: Dover.

Bhumicitr, Vatcharin
1988. *The Taste of Thailand.* Bangkok: Asia Books.

Butel, Jane
1987. *Hotter than Hell.* Tucson: HP Books.

Callery, Emma, ed.
1991. *The Complete Hot and Spicy Cookbook.* Secaucus, NJ: Wellfleet Press.

Cooper, Joe
1952. *With or without Beans.* Dallas: William S. Henson 1952.

Cranwell, John Phillips
1975. *The Hellfire Cookbook.* New York: Quadrangle.

de Benitez, Ana M.
1974. *Pre-Hispanic Cookbook (Cocina Prehispanica).* Mexico, D.F.: Ediciones Euroamericanas Klaus Thiele.

Dent, Huntley
1985. *The Feast of Santa Fe.* New York: Simon and Schuster.

DeWitt, Dave
1991. *Hot Spots.* Rocklin, CA: Prima Publishing.
1992. *Chile Peppers: A Selected Bibliography of the Capsicums.* Las Cruces, NM: Chile Institute.

DeWitt, Dave, and Paul Bosland
1993. *The Pepper Garden.* Berkeley: Ten Speed Press.

DeWitt, Dave, and Nancy Gerlach
1984. *The Fiery Cuisines.* New York: Street Martin's Press. Berkeley: Ten Speed Press, 1991.
1986. *Fiery Appetizers.* New York: Street Martin's Press. Albuquerque: Border Books, 1991.
1990. *The Whole Chile Pepper Book.* Boston: Little, Brown & Company
1992. *Just North of the Border.* Rocklin, CA: Prima Publishing.

DeWitt, Dave and Arthur Pais
1994. *A World of Curries.* Boston: Little, Brown & Company

DeWitt, Dave and Mary Jane Wilan
1992. *The Food Lover's Handbook to the Southwest.* Rocklin, CA: Prima Publishing.
1993. *Callaloo, Calypso, and Carnival: The Cuisines of Trinidad and Tobago.* Freedom, CA: Crossing Press.

DeWitt, Dave, Mary Jane Wilan, and Melissa T. Stock
1994. *Hot & Spicy & Meatless.* Rocklin, CA: Prima Publishing.
1994. *Hot & Spicy Chili.* Rocklin, CA: Prima Publishing.

Duncan, Geraldine
1985. *Some Like It Hotter.* San Francisco: 101 Productions.

Duong, Binh, and Marcia Kiesel
1991. *Simple Art of Vietnamese Cooking.* New York: Prentice-Hall.

Halasz, Zoltan
1963. *Hungarian Paprika Through the Ages.* Budapest: Corvina Press.

Harris, Dunstan
1988. *Island Cooking: Recipes from the Caribbean.* Freedom, CA: Crossing Press

Harris, Jessica
1985. *Hot Stuff: A Cookbook in Praise of the Piquant.* New York: Atheneum. (Also, Ballantine, 1986.)
1992. *Tasting Brazil.* New York: Macmillan.

Hatchen, Harva
1970. *Kitchen Safari.* New York: Atheneum.

Hazen-Hammon, Susan
1993. *Chile Pepper Fever: Mine's Hotter than Yours.* Stillwater, MN: Voyageur Press.

Hodgson, Moira
1977. *The Hot and Spicy Cookbook.* New York: McGraw-Hill.

Jamison, Cheryl Alters and Bill Jaminson
1991. *The Rancho de Chimayó Cookbook.* Boston: Harvard Common Press.

Karoff, Barbara
1989. *South American Cooking.* Berkeley, CA: Aris Books.

Kennedy, Diana
1972. *The Cuisines of Mexico.* New York: Harper and Row.
1975. *The Tortilla Book.* New York: Harper and Row.
1978. *Recipes from the Regional Cooks of Mexico.* New York: Harper and Row.

Lomeli, Arturo
1986. *El Chile y Otros Picantes.* Mexico, D.F.: Asociacion Mexicana de Estudios para la Defensa del Comsumidor.

Long-Solis, Janet
1986. *Capsicum y Cultura: La Historia del Chilli.* Mexico, D.F.: Fondo de Cultura Economica.

Marks, Copeland
1985. *False Tongues and Sunday Bread: A Guatemalan and Mayan Cookbook.* New York: M. Evans
1989. *The Exotic Kitchens of Indonesia.* New York: M. Evans

McDermott, Nancie
1992. *Real Thai.* San Francisco: Chronicle Books.

McMahan, Jacqueline
1987. *The Salsa Book.* Lake Hughes, CA: Olive Press.
1987. *Red and Green Chile Book.* Lake Hughes, CA: Olive

Miller, Mark
1991. *The Great Chile Book.* Berkeley: Ten Speed Press.
1994. *The Great Salsa Book.* Berkeley: Ten Speed Press.

Murphy, Rosalea
1988. *The Pink Adobe Cookbook.* New York: Dell.

Naj, Amal
1992. *Peppers: A Story of Hot Pursuits.* New York: Knopf.

Ortiz, Elizabeth Lambert
1968. *The Complete Book of Mexican Cooking.* New York: Bantam.
1973. *The Complete Book of Caribbean Cooking.* New York: M. Evans & Company
1979. *The Book of Latin American Cooking.* New York: Knopf.

Owen, Sri
1980. *Indonesian Food and Cookery.* London: Prospect Books.
Palazuelos, Susana, et al.
1991. *Mexico The Beautiful Cookbook.* San Francisco: Collins.

Peyton, James W.
1990. *El Norte: The Cuisine of Northern Mexico.* Santa Fe: Red Crane Books.
1994. *La Cocina de La Frontera: Mexican-American Cooking from the Southwest.* Santa Fe: Red Crane Books.

Purseglove, J. W., et al.
1981. *"Chillies: Capsicum spp."* In *Spices.* London: Longman's.

Quintana, Patricia
1986. *The Taste of Mexico.* New York: Stewart, Tabori, and Chang.
1989. *Mexico's Feasts of Life.* Tulsa: Council Oak Books.

Ries, M.
1968. *The Hundred-Year History of Tabasco.* Avery Island, LA: McIlhenny Company

Schlesinger, Chris, and John Willoughby
1990. *The Thrill of the Grill.* New York: William Morrow.
1993. *Salsas, Sambals, Chutneys and Chowchows.* New York: William Morrow
1994. *Big Flavors of the Hot Sun.* New York: William Morrow

Schweid, R.
1980. *Hot Peppers (Tabasco).* Seattle: Madronna Publishing.

Solomon, Charmaine
1976. *The Complete Asian Cookbook.* New York: McGraw-Hill.

Solomon, Jay
1990. *Chutneys, Relishes, and Table Sauces.* Freedom, CA: Crossing Press.
1991. *A Taste of the Tropics.* Freedom, CA: Crossing Press.
1994. *Global Grilling.* Freedom, CA: Crossing Press.

Somos, Andras
1984. *The Paprika.* Budapest: Akademiai Kaido.

Stendahl
1979. *Spicy Food.* New York: Holt, Rinehart, and Winston.

Tarantino, Jim
1992. *Marinades.* Freedom, CA: Crossing Press

Tolbert, F. X.
1972. *A Bowl of Red.* New York: Doubleday.

Thompson, Jennifer Trainer
1994. *Hot Licks.* San Francisco: Chronicle Books.

Warren, William, et al.
1992. *Thailand the Beautiful Cookbook.* San Francisco: CollinsPublishers.

Willinsky, Helen
1990. *Jerk: Barbecue from Jamaica.* Freedom, CA: Crossing Press.

Wolfe, Linda
1970. *The Cooking of the Caribbean Islands.* New York: Time-Life Books.

Mail-Order Catalogs

These are the main mail-order suppliers of the hot and spicy products called for in this cookbook.

Blazing Chile Bros.
(800) 473-9040

Chile Pepper Magazine
P.O. Box 80780
Albuquerque, NM 87198
(800) 359-1483

Chile Today, Hot Tamale
919 Highway 33, Suite 47
Freehold, JN 07728
(800) 468-7377

Colorado Spice Company
5030 Nome Street, Unit A
Denver, CO 80239
(303) 373-0141

Coyote Cocina
1364 Rufina Circle #1
Santa Fe, NM 87501
(800) 866-HOWL

Dean and DeLuca
Mail Order Department
560 Broadway
New York, NY 10012
(212) 431-1691

Don Alfonso Foods
P.O. Box 201988
Austin, TX 78720
(800) 456-6100

Enchanted Seeds
P.O. Box 6087
Las Cruces, NM 88006
(505) 233-3033

Flamingo Flats
Box 441
St. Michael's, MD 21663
(800) 468-8841

Frieda's, Inc.
P.O. Box 584888
Los Angeles, CA 90058
(800) 421-9477

GMB Specialty Foods, Inc.
Norma Bishop Mustard & Sauces
Scottsdale Mustard Co.
Gourmet Mustard Co.
P.O Box 962
San Juan Capistrano, CA 92693-0962
(714) 240-3053

Hot Sauce Club of America
P.O. Box 687
Indian Rocks Beach
FL 34635-0687
(800) SAUCE-2-U
Ft. Lauderdale, FL 33307

Hot Sauce Harry's
The Dallas Farmer's Market
3422 Flair Drive
Dallas, Texas 75229
(214) 902-8552

Le Saucier
Faneuil Hall Marketplace
Boston, MA 02109
(617) 227-9649

Lotta Hotta
3150 Mercier, Ste. 516
Kansas City, MO 64111
(816) 931-6700

Melissa's World Variety Produce
P.O. Box 21127
Los Angeles, CA 90021
(800) 468-7111

Mo Hotta, Mo Betta
P.O. Box 4136
San Luis Obispo, CA 93403
(800) 462-3220

Nancy's Specialty Market
P.O. Box 327
Wye Mills, MD 21679
(800) 462-6291

Old Southwest Trading Company
P.O. Box 7545
Albuquerque, NM 87194
(505) 836-0168

Pendery's
304 East Belknap
Fort Worth, TX 76102
(800) 533-1879

Pepper Gal
P.O. Box 23006
Ft. Lauderdale, FL 33307
(305) 537-5540

Pepper Joe's, Inc.
7 Tyburn Court
Timonium, MD 21093
(410) 561-8158

Santa Fe School of Cooking
116 W. San Francisco Street
Santa Fe, NM 87501
(505) 983-4511

Shepherd's Garden Seeds
6116 Highway 9
Felton, CA 95018
(408) 335-6910

South Side Pepper Co.
320 N. Walnut Street
Mechanicsburg, PA 17055
(717) 691-7132

Retail Shops

Here are the retail shops or markets that specialize in hot and spicy products. Some of them have mail-order catalogs. It has been difficult to keep up with the explosion in hot shop retailers, so we apologize if we have missed any. For shops listed with post office boxes, call first for directions to their location.

Calido Chile Traders
5360 Merriam Drive
Merrian, KS 66203
(913) 384-0019
(800) 568-8468

Caribbean Spice Company
2 S. Church Street
Fairhope, AL 36532
(800) 990-6088

Central Market
4001 N. Lamar
Austin, TX 78756
(512) 206-1000

Chile Hill Emporium
Box 9100
Bernalillo, NM 87004
(505) 867-3294

The Chile Shop
109 East Water Street
Santa Fe, NM 87501
(505) 983-6080

Chili Patch U.S.A.
204 San Felipe N.W.
Albuquerque, NM 87104
(505) 242-4454; (800) 458-0646

Chili Pepper Emporium
328 San Felipe NW
Albuquerque, NM 87104
(505) 242-7538

Chili Pepper Mania
1709-F Airline Hwy., P.O. Box 232
Hollister, CA 95023
(408) 636-8259

Chutneys
143 Delaware Street
Lexington, OH 44904
(419) 884-2853

Colorado Spice Company
5030 Nome Street, Unit A
Denver, CO 80239
(303) 373-0141; (800) 67-SPICE

Coyote Cafe General Store
132 West Water Street
Santa Fe, NM 87501
(505) 982-2454; (800) 866-HOWL

Dat'l Do-It Hot Shop
P.O. Box 4019
St. Augustine, FL 32085
(904) 824-5303; (800) HOT-DATL

Dat'l Do-It Hot Shop
Dadeland Mall
7535 North Kendall Drive
Miami, FL 37211
(305) 253-0248

Down Island Ventures
P.O. Box 37
Cruz Bay, St. John, U.S. Virgin Islands
(809) 693-7000

Eagle Mountain Gifts
634 S. China Lake Boulevard
Ridgecrest, CA 93555
(619) 375-3071

Fiery Foods
909 20th Avenue South
Nashville, TN 37212
(615) 320-5475

Free Spirit
420 S. Mill Avenue
Tempe, AZ 85281
(602) 966-4339

Gourmet Gallery
320N. Hwy. 89A
Singua Plaza
Sedona, AZ 86336

Garden Gate Gift Shop
Tucson Botanical Gardens
2150 North Alvernon Way
Tucson, AZ 85712
(602) 326-9686

GMB Specialty Foods, Inc.
P.O. Box 962
San Juan Capistrano, CA 92693-0962
(714) 240-3053

Hatch Chile Express
P.O. Box 350
Hatch, NM 87937
(505) 267-3226

Hell's Kitchen
216 Lipincott Avenue
Riverside, NJ 08075
(609) 764-1487

Hell's Kitchen
Pennsasken Mart—Store #328
Route #130
Pennsasken, NJ 08019
(609) 764-1330

Hot Hot Hot
56 South Delacey Ave.
Pasadena, CA 91105
(818) 564-1090
(800) 959-7742
e-mail hothothot@ Earthlink.net
URL http://www.hot.presence.com/hot/

Hot Kicks
4349 Raymir Place
Wauwatosa, WI 53222
(414) 536-7808

Hot Licks
P.O. Box 7854
Hollywood, FL 33081
(305) 987-7105

Hot Lovers Fiery Foods
1282 Wolseley Avenue
Winnipeg, Manitoba R3G 1H4
(204) 772-6418

Hot Papa's Fiery Flavors
11121 Weeden Road
Randolph, NY 14772
(716) 358-4302

The Hot Spot
5777 South Lakeshore Dr.
Shreveport, LA 71119
(318) 635-3581

The Hot Spot
1 Riverfront Plaza #300
Lawrence, KS 66044
(913) 841-7200

Hot Stuff
288 Argonne Avenue
Long Beach, CA 90803
(310) 438-1118

Hot Stuff
227 Sullivan Street
New York, NY 10012
(212) 254-6120; (800) 466-8206

Hots for You—
Chili Pepper Emporium
8843 Shady Meadow Drive
Sandy, UT 84093
(801) 255-7800

Jones and Bones
621 Capitola Avenue
Capitola, CA 95010
(408) 462-0521

Le Saucier
Faneuil Hall Marketplace
Boston, MA 02109
(617) 227-9649

Lotta Hotta
3150 Mercier, Suite 516
Kansas City, MO 64111
(816) 931-6700

The Original Hot Sauce Company
Avenue of Shops
1421-C Larimer Street
Denver, CO 80202
(303) 615-5812

New Orleans
School of Cooking
620 Decatur Street
New Orleans, LA 70130
(504) 482-3632

Pampered Pirate
4 Norre Gade
St. Thomas, U.S. Virgin Islands 00802
(809) 775-5450

Peppers
2009 Highway 1
Dewey Beach, DE 19971
(302) 227-1958; (800) 998-3473

Pepperhead Hot Shoppe
7036 Kristi Court
Garner, NC 27529
(919) 553-4576

Pepper Joe's, Inc.
7 Tyburn Court
Timonium, MD 21093
(410) 561-8158

Potpourri
303 Romero NW
Plaza Don Luis, Old Town
Albuquerque, NM 87104
(505) 243-4087

Pungent Pod
25 Haviland Road
Queensbury, NY 12804
(518) 793-3180

Rivera's Chile Shop
109 1/2 Concho Street
San Antonio, TX 78207
(210) 226-9106

Salsas, Etc.!
3683 Tunis Avenue
San Jose, CA 95132
(408) 263-6392

Salsas, Etc.!
374 Eastridge Mall
San Jose, CA 95122
(408) 223-9020

Sambet's Cajun Store
8644 Spicewood Springs Road, Suite F
Austin, TX 78759
(800) 472-6238

Santa Fe Emporium
104 W. San Francisco
Santa Fe, NM 87501
(505) 984-1966

Santa Fe School of Cooking
116 West San Francisco Street
Santa Fe, NM 87501
(505) 983-4511

Santa Fe Trading Company
7 Main Street
Tarrytown, NY 10591
(914) 332-1730

Señor Chile's at Rawhide
23020 North Scottsdale Road
Scottsdale, AZ 85255
(602) 563-5600

Sherwood's Lotsa Hotsa
P.O. Box 2106
Lakeside, CA 92040
(619) 443-7982

Some Like It Hot
3208 Scott Street
San Francisco, CA 94123
(415) 441-7HOT

Some Like It Hot
301 S. Light Street
Harbor Place
Baltimore, MD 21202
(410) 547-2HOT

Cookbook Sources

A Southern Season
Eastgate Shopping Center
P.O. Box 2678
Chapel Hill, NC 27515
(800) 253-3663

**The Stonewall
Chili Pepper Company**
P.O. Box 241
Stonewall, TX 78671
(210) 644-2667; (800) 232-2995

Sunbelt Shows
P.O. Box 4980
Albuquerque, NM 87196
(505) 873-9103

**Sunny Caribbee
Spice Company**
P.O. Box 3237
St. Thomas, U.S. Virgin Islands
   00803
(809) 494-2178

Tabasco Country Store
Avery Island, LA 70513
(318) 365-8173

Tabasco Country Store
Riverwalk Marketplace
1 Poydras Street
New Orleans, LA 70130
(504) 523-1711

**Uncle Bill's
House of Hot Sauce**
311 N. Higgins Avenue
Missoula, MT 59801
(406) 543-5627

The Whole Earth Grainery
111 Ivinson Avenue
Laramie, WY 82070
(307) 745-4268

Books for Cooks
301 South Light Street
Baltimore, MD 21202
(410) 547-9066

Canyonlands Publications
Karen Price and Brian Billideau
4999 E. Empire, Unit A
Flagstaff, AZ 86004
(602) 527-0730
Fax (602) 527-1873
Distributor of Southwestern
cookbooks.

Chronicle Books
Chris Boral
275 5th Street
San Francisco, CA 94103
(415) 777-8838

The Cook's Bookshop
3854 Fifth Avenue
San Diego, CA 92103
(619) 296-3636

The Cooks Library
8373 W. Third Street
Los Angeles, CA 90048
(213) 655-3141

The Crossing Press
Dennis Hayes, marketing director
P.O. Box 1048
Freedom, CA 95019
(800) 777-1048
Publisher of cookbooks, including
several dedicated to the fiery
foods lover.

Golden West Publishers
Bruce Fisher
4113 N. Longview
Phoenix, AZ 85014
(602) 265-4392
Fax (602) 279-6901
Publisher of Southwestern
cookbooks.

Homestyle Books (mail-order only)
Book-of-the-Month Club Division
1225 South Market Street
Mechanicsburg, PA 17055
(717) 697-1301

Hoppin' Johns
30 Pinckney Street
Charleston, SC 29401
(803) 578-6404

Kitchen Arts & Letters
1435 Lexington Avenue
New York, NY 10128
(212) 876-5550

Powells Books for Cooks
3739 S.E. Hawthorne Blvd.
Portland, OR 97214

Ten Speed Press
Phil Wood and Jo Ann Deck
P.O. Box 7123
Berkeley, CA 94707
(510) 845-8414
Fax (510) 524-1052
Publisher of Southwest cookbooks,
books on chiles, and chile posters.

Manufacturers

This is not a complete listing of hot and spicy food manufacturers (who number well over a thousand), but rather a listing of those represented by recipes in this book, plus other exhibitors in the recent Fiery Foods Shows.

Adams Farm
Jeanne Adams
Route 4, Box 391
Canton, TX 75103
(903) 479-3609
Manufacturer of potpourri from chiles and assorted products.

Adeline's Gourmet Foods
Adeline Reyes
611 N. La Brea Avenue
Los Angeles, CA 90036
(213) 933-9959
Fax (213) 933-9976
Manufacturer of gourmet salsas: mango, kiwi, and coconut.

Ai Kan Company
Sue Louie
903 South 8th Street
Colorado Springs, CO 80906
(719) 632-3607

The Alder Market
Wayne Doerr
P.O. Box 469
Stockton, CA 95201
(209) 467-4822, Fax (209) 467-4826
Manufacturer of salad dressings.

All Cajun Food Company
Stan Gauthier
1019 Delcambre Road
Breaux Bridge, LA 70517
(318) 332-3613
Manufacturer of barbecue sauces, Cajun Hot Sauce, and Cajun Chow Chow.

Amy Stein Art
Amy Stein
510 Sunset Street, Apt. 2
Santa Fe, NM 87501
(505) 983-2069
Artist specializing in fine art renderings and posters of chiles.

Andy's Good 'n Hot Stuff
Andy Burkhardt
P.O. Box 284
D'Lo, MS 39062
(601) 847-4663
Manufacturer of hot tomato salsas, mustards, barbecue sauces, and green chile salsa.

Anjo's Imports
Lloyd and Valerie Webster
P.O. Box 4031
Cerritos, CA 90703
(310) 865-9544
Fax: (310) 865-9544
Importer of Jamaican Habanero hot sauces and jerk seasoning.

Anne's Country Cupboard
Ann Hillmeyer
62 Derek Road
Sandia Park, NM 87047
(505) 281-1159

Antilleo Foods
Victoria and Leander Hamilton
6080 Chabot Road
Oakland, CA 94618
(510) 450-0123, (510) 601-0227
Manufacturer and importer of Spitfire Red Pepper Sauce from Barbados, West Indies.

Apecka Peppered Pickles
Sharon Eisenbraun
9802 Coldwater Circle
Dallas, TX 75228
(214) 321 8219

ATEX Products and Exporting, Inc.
James Divine
P.O. Box 80633
Midland, TX 79708
(915) 699-4568
Wholesale and institutional dry spice and vegetable mixes.

Atomic Bob's
Jeff Williams
1016 S. Dwight
Pampa, TX 79065
(806) 665-7755
Manufacturer of barbecue sauces.

Baja Originals
Mike Marzio and Steve Marzio
9625 Black Mountain Road, #204
San Diego, CA 92126
(619) 695-9435
Fax (619) 695-9827
Manufacturer of salsa and chip bowls.

Bee Torgerson, Food Rep
Bee Torgerson
3546 Vista Grande NW
Albuquerque, NM 87120
(505) 839-0630
Sales representative for Rothschild's Raspberry Farms, El Paso Chile Company, Just Off Melrose.

Blazing Oregon Food Products
Tim Fex
1430 Willamette Street, Suite 17
Eugene, OR 97401
(503) 683-1079
Fax (503) 686-9329
Manufacturer of spicy snacks.

Bowman's Landing Epicurean Company
Stacy Tanner
605 E. Chicago Avenue
Hinsdale, IL 60521
(800) VINEGAR
Manufacturer of mustards, pastas, two chile-infused vinegars
(Chicago Fire and Jazzy Ginger), and Gusty Garni vinegar.

The Brown Adobe, Inc.
Julienne V. Brown
200 Lincoln Avenue, Suite 130
Phoenixville, PA 19460
(215) 935-8588
(800) 392-2041 (for orders only)
Fax (215) 935-3484
Manufacturer of salsas, sauces, and other spicy specialties, including Holy Habanero.

Bueno Foods, Inc.
Abe Valdez
2001 4th Street S.W.
Albuquerque, NM 87102
(505) 243-2722
Fax (505) 242-1680
For over 40 years, a manufacturer of New Mexican food products, including frozen entrées.

Bullfrog Enterprises
Mack & Beth Jordan
P. O. Box 92485
Albuquerque, NM 87199-2485
(505) 897-9556

Busha Browne
Winston Stona
P. O. Box 386
Newport East, Kingston, Jamaica
West Indies
(809) 922-1989
Fax (809) 922-1566

Byron's Catering
Scott Landry
425 Seventh Street
Lake Charles, LA 70601
(800) 297-6670
Manufacturer of Louisiana spice products.

C&C Enterprises
Wanda Clark and Phil Clark
P.O. Box 30041
Albuquerque, NM 87190
(505) 881-4921
Manufacturer of Fiesta barbecue sauces: green chile, red chile, and cayenne.

Cafe Terra Cotta
Donald Luria and Donna Nordin
4310 N. Campbell Avenue
Tucson, AZ 85718
(602) 577-8181
Manufacturer of Southwestern spice mixes, salsas, salad dressings, and spreads.

Cajun Rush Pepper Sauce
Rush Biossat
22295 Gull Street
Maurepas, LA 70449
(504) 695-6692
Manufacturer of Cajun Rush Pepper Sauce.

California-Antilles Trading Company
Richard Gardner
3446 Wilshire Terrace
San Diego, CA 92104
(619) 295-6481
Fax (619) 295-6481
Importer of West Indies Creole Gourmet Hot Pepper Sauce.

Cannon Unlimited
John and Diane Cannon
2724 Tennessee NE
Albuquerque, NM 87110
(505) 294-7018
Manufacturer of Cannon's Sweet Hot products, including green chile salsa, specialty red salsa, and jalapeño salsa.

Caribbean Food Products, Inc.
Mary Jane Barnes, Robert Barnes, and Carl Nelson
1936 N. Second Street
Jacksonville Beach, FL 32250
(904) 246-0149
Fax (904) 246-7273
Manufacturer and importer of Trinidad Habanero Pepper Sauce.

Carmen's of New Mexico USA
Bonnie Samuel
401 Mountain Road NW
Albuquerque, NM 87102
(505) 842-5119
Manufacturer of salsas, chile and habanero chile powders, and blue-corn products.

Cedar Hill Seasonings
Felicia Shaefer
P. O Box 4055
Edmond, OK 73083
(405) 340-1119

Century Sauce Kitchens
Kathleen Redle
P.O. Box 4057
Copley, OH 44321
(216) 666-2578
Fax (216) 666-1768
Manufacturer of hot pepper sauces.

Chef's Choice
Tom Hill
P.O. Box 134
Upper Sandusky, OH 43351
(419) 294-5605
Fax (419) 294-5522

Chia I Foods, Ltd.
Dien Ly
1711 Floradale Avenue
South El Monte, CA 91733
(818) 401-3095
Fax (818) 401-9519
Importer, bulk distributor, and wholesaler of dried Chinese red chile pods,

Chile Bravo! Imports
Angel Sustaeta
2719 West French
San Antonio, TX 78201
(210) 732-7943
Importer of Mexican Avante chipotle chiles.

Chile Master, Inc.
Pete Giadone
743 Lane 24
Pueblo, CO 81006
(719) 543-5204

Chile Pepper Magazine
Robert Spiegel, publisher
P.O. Box 80780
Albuquerque, NM 87198
(505) 266-8322
Publisher of Chile Pepper, the magazine of spicy world cuisine.

Chile Today, Hot Tamale
919 Highway 33, Suite 47
Freehold, JN 07728
(800) 468-7377

Chugwater Chili Corporation
Marcelyn Brown
210 First Street, P.O. Box 92
Chugwater, WY 82210
(307) 422-3345
Fax (307) 422-3357
Manufacturer of Chugwater Chili Mix, Chili Dip, and Dressing Mix.

Clove 'n Vine
Diane Trenhaile
17500 S.W. Oldsville Road
McMinnville, OR 97128
(503) 843-2183
Manufacturer of elephant garlic food products and wreaths.

Colorado Salsa Company
Bonny Griffith
P. O. Box 621975
Littleton, CO 80162
(303) 932-2617

Coyote Cocina
Dave Hoemann
1364 Rufina Circle #1
Santa Fe, NM 87501
(800) 866-HOWL
Fax (505) 473-3100
Manufacturer of Coyote Cocina salsas, chile-flavored honeys, hot sauces, and dried chiles.

Crazy Cajun Enterprises
Charley Addison
P.O. Box 426
Petaluma, CA 94953
(707) 769-8515 Fax (707) 769-9185
Manufacturer of Crazy Cajun gourmet sauces, salsas, and gumbo.

Crazy Ed's BM Brewery
Ed Chilleen
P. O. Box 1940
Cave Creek, AZ 85331
(602) 254-8579

Creative Chef Foods
Fred Fatino
14406 W. 100th Street
Lenexa, KS 66215
(913) 492-1414
Manufacturer of extremely hot habanero sauce, habanero jelly, and barbecue sauce.

Dave's Gourmet
David Hirschkopf
3350 Laguna, Suite 201
San Francisco, CA 94123
(800) 758-0372
Manufacturer of Insanity Sauce and other very hot chile products.

Deneen & Company
Greg Deneen
1590 San Mateo Lane
Santa Fe, NM 87501
(505) 988-1515

Desert Farms
Virginia Prochaska
3902 Lila
Las Cruces, NM 88005
(505) 523-9537

Desert Gardens
Mark Harden
P.O. Box 1777
Tijeras, NM 87059
(505) 281-7698
Producer of hot and spicy dip mixes and spice blends.

Desert Rose Foods, Inc.
1955 West Grant Road
Suite 215
Tucson, AZ 85745

Don Alfonso Foods
José Marmolejo
P.O. Box 201988
Austin, TX 78720
(800) 456-6100
Fax (512) 335-0636
Manufacturer of Mole Sauce, Chipotles in Adobo Sauce, Tomatillo-Chipotle Salsa, and other sauces.

Eddie's Cajun Flavors, Inc.
Eddie Adams
5809 Juan Tabo NE
Albuquerque, NM 87111
(505) 293-2922
Fax (505) 828-9496
Manufacturer of Cajun spice blends for seasoning meats and seafood.

Edmunds Enterprises
Tom Edmunds
820 Cypress Avenue
Hermosa Beach, CA 90254
(310) 379-5572

El Norteño Restaurant
Leo Nuñez
7306 Zuni N.E.
Albuquerque, NM 87108
(505) 256-1431
A restaurant offering foods of northern Mexico.

Excelsior Trading Company, Inc.
Raymond Chai-Chang
7980 N.W. 67th Street
Miami, FL 33166
(305) 594-1142
Distributor of Gray's Jamaican
Hot Pepper Sauce and Jamaican
Spicy Sauce.

Firehouse Bar & Grill
Dylan Moore
1525 Blake Street
Denver, CO 80202
(303) 820-3308

FoFo's Caribbean Spice
FoFo Voltaire
109 San Pablo S.E.
Albuquerque, NM 87108
(505) 255-3925
Manufacturer of Caribbean spice
blends and dip mixes.

Frank & Bryan Foods, Inc.
Frank Laux
22820 Highway 45 North, 1-N
Spring, TX 77373
(713) 355-1786
Manufacturer of Sunsalsa products,
including salsas, quesos, and frijoles.

Frog Ranch Foods
Craig Cornett
P. O. Box 25
Millfield, OH 45761
(614) 797-3126

Garcia's Gourmet
Roberto Garcia
P.O. Box 2001
Watsonville, CA 95077
(408) 722-4453
Manufacturer of pickled garlic,
jalapeños and carrots, and flavored
vinegars and oils.

Garlic Grocery
Tim Felice or Carissa
7888 Wren Avenue, D-143
Gilroy, CA 95020
(408) 842-3330
Manufacturer of mustard, salsa,
dressing, oil, and garlic braids.

Gator Hammock
Buddy Taylor
P.O. Box 360
Felda, FL 33930
(813) 675-0687 (800) 66-GATOR
All-natural hot sauce and Gator Que
barbecue sauce.

Giadone Farms
Pete and Joyce Giadone
743 Lane 24
Pueblo, CO 81006
(719) 543-5204
Chile growers with limited supplies
of frozen green chiles; manufacturers
of self-peeling chile roasters.

Gil's Gourmet Gallery
Steffanie Porter and Gil Tortolani
637 Ortiz, Suite B
Sand City, CA 93955
(408) 394-3305
Fax (408) 394-9144
Manufacturer of habanero and habanero-
flavored garlic-stuffed olives, salsas, and
flavored cashews, and pistachios.

G. L. Mezzetta, Inc.
Dale Lucas
1201 E. MacArthur Street
Sonoma, CA 95476
(707) 938-8388
Fax (707) 938-8304
Manufacturer of pickled peppers and
related specialties, including prepared
horseradish, salsas, and hot sauces.

Goldwater's Foods of Arizona
Carolyn Ross
P.O. Box 9846
Scottsdale, AZ 85252
(602) 966-4667
Fax (602) 966-7012
Manufacturer of Southwestern
salsas, sauces, and chili mix.

Gourmet Creations
Debra Wilmot
P.O. Box 7310
Albuquerque, NM 87194
(505) 869-5605
Fax (505) 869-4235
Manufacturer of hot chile oil,
chile jellies, and salsa.

Gourmet Gear
2320 Abbot Kinney
Venice, CA 90291
(800) 682-4635
Fax (310) 301-4115

Great Bison Spice and Trading Company
Buffalo Bob Cahill
P.O. Box 2573
Sparks, NV 89432
(702) 359-0144
Manufacturer of blended
dry seasonings.

The Great Southwest Spice Company
Laura Deck
2103 18th Avenue S.
Nashville, TN 37212
(615) 292-1355
Manufacturer of dry chili spices,
a sweet and smoky marinade,
and a barbecue rub.

The Grocery Emporium
David Bromberg
1403 Girard N.E.
Albuquerque, NM 87106
(505) 265-6771
Manufacturer of green chile turkey
sausage.

Gunpowder Foods, Inc.
Bruce Pinnell
P.O. Box 293
Texas, MD 21030
(410) 692-6874
Fax (410) 557-8549
Manufacturer of Gunpowder Gourmet
Texas Chili Mix.

Heart of the Desert Pistachios
Marianne Schweers
7288 Highway 70
Alamogordo, NM 88310
(505) 434-0035
Fax (505) 434-2132
Producer of pistachio products from
New Mexico-grown nuts, including hot
and spicy pistachios.

Heat Wave Hot Sauce
Theresa N. O'Hara
Box 5564
Street Thomas, U.S. Virgin Islands 00803
(809) 777-9289
Manufacturer of Heat Wave Hot Sauce.

Hi-Co Western Products
Andy Housholder
1806 East Main Street
Mesa, AZ 85203
(602) 834-0149
Fax (602) 833-1374
Manufacturer of Hogg Wild Chili
Fixings and Fiesta Shaker.

Hogtowne Bar-B-Que Sauce
Chuck Kinard
P. O. Box 13233
Gainesville, FL 32604
(904) 375-6969

Hot Heads, Inc.
Ken Roda and Wendy Roda
639 East Marion Street
Lancaster, PA 17602
(717) 396-9784
Distributor of hot sauces from around
the world and producer of Hot Heads
hot sauce products.

Hot Sauce Harry's
Bob Harris
3422 Flair Drive
Dallas, TX 75229
(214) 902-8552

House of Seagram
Dave Tethal
6731 Academy NE, Suite 16
Albuquerque, NM 87109
(505) 822-8535

Indel Food Products, Inc.
Anabel Rodriguez
11415 Cedar Oak Drive
El Paso, TX 79936
(915) 590-5914

The Imagination Association
E. J. Tobin
10477 Pearson Place
Shadow Hills, CA 91040
(818) 353-0840

International Bar-B-Q
Morris Souders
P.O. Box 1370
Nashville, TN 47448
(812 988-6150
Food buyers catalog for exporting
food products

**Isla Vieques
Condiment Company**
Diana Starke and Jim Starke
P.O. Box 1496
Vieques, Puerto Rico 00765
(809) 741-0848
Fax (809) 741-2700
Manufacturer of hot sauces, mustards,
and tropical condiments including chutney.

Island Gourmet
Louis Olive
8736 S.W. 72nd Street
Miami, FL 33137
(305) 596-7300
Manufacturer of Island Gourmet
Jamaican Marinade.

Island Imports
Francis Hamilton
P.O. Box 78925
Los Angeles, CA 90016
(213) 732-6320
Manufacturer of Evadney's All-Purpose
Jamaican Hot Sauce and habanero
products.

JOT Products Company
Doug Conklin
13503 M. L. King Way S. #A-212
Seattle, WA 98178-5179
(206) 277-1669

Jilli Pepper, Inc.
Jill Levin
P.O. Box 7546
Albuquerque, NM 87194
(505) 344-0415
Manufacturer of fresh salsas; tropical,
red chile, and green chile.

Jo B's
Joseph Brent
Box 316
Warren, VT 05674
(802) 496-4202

Jones Productions
Trish Jones
P.O. Box 362
Key West, FL 33041
(305) 296-1863
Manufacturer of Big John's Famous Key
West Hot Sauce.

Joy's of Colorado
Joy Kyzer
187 Redman Lane CR 302
Durango, CO 81301
(303) 259-2483
Manufacturer of chile jellies and honey-
bean soup.

KAL International
Joe Lipwin
P.O. Box 482
Hollis, NH 03049
(603) 465-2428
Fax (603) 465-2481
Importer of Jamaican scotch bonnet
chiles.

Kasemir Foods, Inc.
Victor Kasemir
100 W. Chestnut, #2904
Chicago, IL 60610
(312) 664-5015
Manufacturer of Vic's spicy foods,
sauces, and relishes.

Kiwi Dundee
Mari Jo Honeycutt and Robert Vigie
P.O. Box 11276
Albuquerque, NM 87192
(505) 237-2135
Importer of foods from Australia
and New Zealand; fruits, chutneys,
and kiwi products.

Lahner Imports, Inc.
Peter Lahner
1056 Tahoe Boulevard, P.O. Box 8389
Incline Village, NV 89452
(702) 831-1223
Fax (702) 831-1528
Importer of hot Hungarian
paprika products.

Leafy Green Dreams
John Weeks
P.O. Box 7
Sky Forest, CA 92385
(909) 337-0616
Manufacturer of chile t-shirts, greeting
cards, jewelry, bean bags, and craft
objects.

Lee Kum Kee, Inc.
Grace Chow
304 South Date Avenue
Alhambra, CA 91803
(818) 282-0337 Fax (818) 282-3425
Manufacturer and importer of Panda
chile sauces and other Asian products.

Leona's Foods, Inc.
Roy Trujillo
P.O. Box 579
Chimayo, NM 87522
(505) 351-4660
Manufacturer of tortillas (white, whole
wheat, and flavored), vegetarian tamales,
and salsas.

Los Dos, Inc.
Jeffrey Gerlach
P.O. Box 7548
Albuquerque, NM 87194
(505) 831-9161k
Fax (505) 836-1682
Wholesale distributor of Rick's
Desert Devil Oil and Rica Red
Habanero products.

Lotta Hotta
Joe Polo
3150 Mercier, Suite 516
Kansas City, MO 64111
(816) 931-6700
Fax (816) 931-6779
Manufacturer of salsas, chile con queso,
jerk sauces, dips, and drink mixes.

Mad Coyote Spice Company
Mad Coyote Joe
P.O. Box 1647
Cave Creek, AZ 85331
(602) 488-1985
Manufacturer of salsa mix, the Chile
from Hell, fajita marinade, and more.

**Mahan's Southwest Gourmet
Sauce, Inc.**
Robert Mahan
P.O. Box 26901
El Paso, TX 79926
(915) 584-8598

Manufacturer of Southwestern
barbecue sauces.

Mangum Enterprises
Barbara Mangum
17502 Hwy. 4, P.O. Box 546
Jemez Springs, NM 87025
(505) 829-3956
Manufacturer of dried stews and
bread mixes, and spicy candy, nuts,
and spreads.

Mannon's Foods
Donna Mannon
1665 E. 18th Street, Suite 114
Tucson, AZ
(602) 622-7178
Fax (602) 398-9314
Manufacturer of red chile bread mixes.

McIlhenny Company
Tanna Dooley
General Delivery
Avery Island, LA 70513
(318) 365-8173

MEB Distributing
Mark S. Wong
390 Swift Avenue, Unit 22
South San Francisco, CA 94080
(415) 589-1180
Fax (415) 588-8235
Importer and distributor of Caribbean
sauces and spices, including Pickapeppa
and Busha Browne sauces.

Mexi-Mary
Judy Montgomery
32 Owen Street
Eureka Springs, AR 72632
(501) 253-8732
Fax (501) 253-8539
Manufacturer of Mexi-Mary Natural
Bloody Mary Mix.

Mick's Peppourri
Tadd Mick and Rod Mick
1707 S. 74th Avenue
Yakima, WA 98908
(509) 966-2328
Manufacturer of premium chile
products, including jellies and chutneys.

Monroe's Restaurants
Kathy Diaz
6051 Osuna NE
Albuquerque, NM 87109
(505) 242-1111

Mosquito Coast Pirate's Delight
Glen Bonner
4644 Gandy Boulevard, No. # 7
Tampa, FL 33611
(813) 837-8410

Mrs. Dog's Products
Julie Applegate
P.O. Box 6034
Grand Rapids, MI 49516
(616) 940-1778
Fax (616) 458-9554
Manufacturer of Mrs. Dog's Jamaican
Jerk Sauce, Hot Pepper Sauce, and
Disappearing Mustard.

Muleshoe Pepper Company
Larry Winkler
401 Main
Muleshoe, TX 79347
(806) 272-4703
Fax (806) 272-5688

Murzan, Inc.
Marla Fuller
2909 Langford Road, # 1-700
Norcross, GA 30071
(404) 448-0583
Fax (404) 448-0967
Manufacturer of pumps for the food
processing industry.

National Hot Pepper Association
Betty Payton
400 N.W. 20th Street
Ft. Lauderdale, FL 33311
(305) 565-4972
Fax (305) 566-2208
Provider of 200 varieties of pepper seeds
and manufacturer of chile condiments

**New Mexico Food Producers
and Processors Association**
Mark Hardin
P.O. Box 1777
Tijeras, NM 87059
Promotor of food products made
in New Mexico.

Norman Bishop Mustards
Nina Estes and Carol Norman
P.O. Box 2451
San Jose, CA 95109
(408) 292-1089
Fax (408) 295-0333
Manufacturer of prepared mustards
and mustard sauces.

O. G. Williams, Inc.
Knial K. Williams
P. O. Box 293
Seligman, MO 65745
(501) 631-1415

Oak Hill Farms
Robert Budd
P.O. Box 888302
Atlanta, GA 30356
(404) 452-8828
Manufacturer of Scorned Woman Hot
Sauce, Vidalia Onion Barbecue Sauce,
and other hot sauces.

Old El Paso Foods (Pet, Inc.)
c/o Barnett Brothers Brokerage
Company
Steve Derrick
5001 Ellison NE
Albuquerque, NM 87109
(505) 345-3694
Manufacturer of Old El Paso Picante
Sauce and Tortilla Chips.

Ol' Gringo Chile Products
Lisa Asel
5106 Lost Padre Mine Road
Las Cruces, NM 88001
(505) 521-3253
Manufacturer of red and green chile
sauces, and gift baskets.

Ore-Ida Foods, Inc.
Becky Stover
220 W. Parkcenter Blvd.
Boise, ID 83706
(208) 838-6316

Pedro's Tamales
Barbara Walters
P.O. Box 3571
Lubbock, TX 79452
(800) 522-9531
Fax (806) 745-5833
Manufacturer of Pedro's Tamales,
which combine stone-ground corn
meal, the finest sirloin butts, and
whole chile pods.

The Pepper Plant
Bob Roush
P.O. Box 1119
Atascadero, CA 93423
(805) 466-7387
Fax (805) 466-9314
Manufacturer of Pepper Plant
Hot Sauce, barbecue Sauce, Salsa,
and Seasoning.

Pecos Red Products
Jo Ann Oakman and Jerry Oakman
4715 Strack, Suite 104
Houston, TX 77069
(713) 251-1000
Manufacturer of Pecos Red Chili Mix.

The Pepper Gal
Betty Payton
P.O. Box 23006
Ft. Lauderdale, FL 33307
(305) 537-5540
Fax (305) 566-2208
Provider of more than two hundred
varieties of pepper seeds.

Peppers
Chip Hearn
2009 Highway 1
Dewey Beach, DE 19971
(302) 227-1958 Fax (302) 227-4603
Manufacturer of Awesome Hot Sauce
and Hot Buns at the Beach Sauce.

Phamous Phloyd's, Inc.
Steve Berge
2998 S. Steele Street
Denver, CO 80210
(303) 757-3285
Manufacturer of barbecue sauce, dry
rub, and marinade kits.

Pikled Garlik Company
Judy Knapp
P.O. Box 846
Pacific Grove, CA 93950
(408) 393-1707
Manufacturer of pickled garlic
and salsas.

Pili Pepper
GTL, Inc.
112 Rittenhouse Street N.W.
Washington, D.C. 20011
(202) 723-6225
Manufacturer of Pili Hot Pepper
Condiment.

Prairie Harvest Spice Products
Regina Spriggs
6863 Birchwood Court N.
Keizer, OR 97303
(503) 390-1984
Manufacturer of salsa products: 3 salsa
dry mixes and 2 shaker jars for pop-
corn and vegetables.

Ring of Fire Hot Sauce
Michael Greening
6755 Mira Mesa Boulevard, Suite 123
#204
San Diego, CA 92121
(619) 549-4809

Rio Grande Chile Company
Anne Tafoya and Tony Gutierrez
P.O. Box 30822
Albuquerque, NM 87190
(505) 883-9037
Fax (505) 883-8424
Manufacturer of red and green chile
jams, jalapeño jam, and taco sauce.

Saguaro Potato Chip Company
Ray Pisciotta and Georgia Pisciotta
860 E. 46th Street
Tucson, AZ 85713
(602) 884-8049
Fax (602) 884-9704
Manufacturer of hot and spicy potato
chips, blue-corn chips, bean dips,
and salsas.

Santa Fe Brand, Inc.
Wayne Scheiner
P.O. Box 8254
Albuquerque, NM 87198
(505) 256-9224
Fax (505) 256-9243
Manufacturer of Santa Fe Brand red
chile pods and chile t-shirts.

Santa Fe Cookie Company
Scot Robinson
1560 Center Drive
Santa Fe, NM 87505
(800) 873-5589
Fax (505) 473-9806
Manufacturer of green chile pretzels
and cookies with chile jelly centers.

Santa Fe Exotix
Todd and Krystyna Sanson
500 N. Guadalupe, De Vargas Center,
Suite G-473
Santa Fe, NM 87501
(505) 988-7063
Fax (505) 982-4789
Manufacturer of Cactus Relish,
Pineapple Salsa, Best o' Pesto and a
new line of exotic, spicy jams.

Santa Fe Ole
Martin Dobyns/Missy Fussell
P.O. Box 2433
Santa Fe, NM 87501
(505) 473-0724

Santa Fe Seasons
Greg Deneen
1590 San Mateo Lane
Santa Fe, NM 87501
(505) 988-1515
Manufacturer of Southwestern
sauces, condiments, and spices,
including Cranberry Especiale
and black bean dip.

Santa Fe Select
Darby Long
369 Montezuma, # 345
Santa Fe, NM 87501
(505) 986-0454
Distributor of gourmet food products
from the Southwest.

Sauces and Salsas, Ltd.
Chuck Evans
7856 Forest Brook Court
Powell, OH 43065
(614) 764-0690
Fax (614) 764-0699
Manufacturer of Montezuma Brand
sauces and salsas.

Sgt. Pepper's
J. P. Hayes
P.O. Box 49565
Austin, TX 78765
(512) 482-0449
Manufacturer of Texas Tears
habanero hot sauce, Southwest Salza,
and Pepper Jazz.

Shepherd's Garden Seeds
Renee Shepherd
6116 Highway 9
Felton, CA 95108
(408) 335-2080
Wholesale, and mail-order supplier of
seeds for the home garden, including
many varieties of chiles.

Silliker Laboratories
Laura Dunn
2100 N. Highway 360, Suite 2006
Grand Prairie, TX 75050
(214) 988-8508

Southwest Seasons Cookbook
Kathryn Godfrey
4901 Calle Alta N.E.
Albuquerque, NM 87111
(505) 296-9448
Publisher of Southwest Seasons
Cookbook, a benefit for the children
of Casa Angelica

Southwest Spirit
Jim and Cynthia Fowler
517 Third Street
Annapolis, MD 21403
(410) 263-4451
Fax (703) 527-7256
Manufacturer of Rio Red Salsa,
Margarita Party Salsa, and Smoked
Black Bean and Corn Salsa.

Spaghetti Western Foods
Julie Feldman
Box 658
Tesuque, NM 87574
(505)753-6409

Spirit Mesa
Jeanne Kyser
126 Shady Oak Circle
Tijeras, NM 87059
(505) 281-7671
Manufacturer of herbal vinegars and
other products.

Starboard Restaurant
Chip Hearn
2009 Highway One
Dewey Beach, DE 19971
(302) 227-4600

Stevens & Associates
Craig Stevens
1576 Minnesota Avenue
San Jose, CA 95125
(408) 978-0608

Stonewall Chili Pepper Company
Jeff Campbell
P.O. Box 241
Stonewall, TX 78671
(800) 232-2995
Producer of Stonewall habanero
products from Texas-grown peppers.

Sumptuous Selections
Mary Lee Wilcox
P.O. Box 457
Rocky Hill, CT 06067
(203) 563-6390
Manufacturer of salsas, pepper jellies,
preserves, and dry spice mixes.

SunWild Foods, Inc.
Kim Wall
P.O. Box 07378
Milwaukee, WI 53207
(414) 298-9950
Manufacturer of Sundance Salsa,
seasonings, and bread mixes.

Taos Mesa Gourmet, Inc.
Me'l Christensen
HCR 74 Box 22203
El Prado, NM 87529
(505) 751-0923

The Tex's Chile Company
Vada Gilreath
P.O. Box 821608
South Florida, FL 33082
(305) 730-7800
Manufacturer of pickled habanero
chiles, spiced pickled garlic, and
jalapeño-stuffed olives.

Thalcash Network
Alois Dogue
11409 E. Evans Avenue
Aurora, CO 80014
(303) 750-2150, (800) 468-0555
Manufacturer of Habanero Hot! Hot!
Hot!, a Panamanian-style pepper sauce.

Tio Tito's Original Mexican Grill
Eddie Stern
2017 Menaul NE
Albuquerque, NM 87107
(505) 883-TITO

T.N.T. Company
Herman Sandoval and Mike Avallone
11113 N. Highway 85
Las Cruces, NM 88005
(505) 524-8915
Fax (505) 525-3589
Manufacturer of T.N.T. chile seasonings.

Trader Rick, Inc.
Rick Engel
339 Saddlebrook Drive
Calhoun, GA 30701
(706) 625-8288
Importer of Barbadian hot sauces.

Tuckie T's, Inc.
Terri Deputy
P.O. Box 31076
Amarillo, TX 79120
(806) 355-4103
Manufacturer of Hotsy Totsy Texas-
style salsa and gift baskets.

Two Chefs
Eric Walton
P.O. Box 101684
Denver, CO 80250
(800) PUR-HELL
Manufacturer of Pure Hell hot sauce.

Uncle Willie's
4003 Raphune Hill, # 501
St. Thomas, U.S. Virgin Islands 00802
(809) 777-4303
Manufacturer of Caribbean-style hot
sauces and rum cakes.

**Upper Mississippi
Sauce Company, Inc.**
Jay Rosenthal
1516 W. Lake Street, #200
Minneapolis, MN 55408
(612) 821-4325
Fax (612) 821-4349
Manufacturer of barbecue sauce.

U.S. Fresh Marketing, Inc.
Jorge Araujo and Tony Battaglia
2304 Wake Forest Street
Virginia Beach, VA 23451
(804) 496-9300
Fax (804) 496-2733
Importer of dried chiles from the
Caribbean.

Virgin Fire
Bob Kennedy
P.O. Box 37
Street John, U.S. Virgin Islands 00831
(809) 694-5937
Manufacturer of Eastern Caribbean
Hot Pepper Sauce, Papaya Fire, and
Pineapple Sizzle.

**Virgin Islands Herb
and Pepper Company**
Richard Reiher
P.O. Box 9519
Street Thomas, Virgin Islands 00801
(809) 776-2145
Manufacturer of habanero paste, curry
garlic sauce, peppered ginger sauce,
steak sauce, and fresh salsa.

Willie B. Famous Designs
Dave and Char DePalma
220 Calamus Meadow Road
Hamden, CT 06514
(203) 281-1807
Manufacturer of chile-design clothing,
tote bags, aprons, towels, and other
products.

Zack's Foods
Jim Akers and John Hurt
20223 Pickering Drive
Belton, MO 64012
(816) 322-3248
Manufacturer of Zack's Virgin
Habanero Sauce, habanero jelly, and
a barbecue and smoking rub.

Zavala Enterprises, Inc.
G. C. Zavala
11816 Mansfied, Bay 1
Spokane, WA 99206
(509) 922-6671
Manufacturer of No Joke Hot Sauce.

Seed Companies

Looking to grow your own? These
companies carry a wide selection of
chile pepper seed varieties.

Enchanted Seeds
PO Box 6087
Las Cruxes, NM 88006
505-233-3033

The Pepper Gal
PO Box 12534
Lake Park, FL 33403

Plants of the Southwest
Agua Fria Route 6, Box 11A
Santa Fe, NM 87501
505-438-8888

Redwood City Seed Co.
Po Box 361
Redwood City, CA 94064
415-325-SEED

Seeds of Change
1364 Rufina Circle #5
Santa Fe, NM 87501
505-983-8956

Shepherd's Garden Seeds
6116 Highway 9
Felton, CA 95018
408-335-6910

Twilley Seed Co.
PO Box 65
Trevose, PA 19053
800-622-SEED

Seed Savers Exchange
Route 3, Box 239
Decorah, IA 52101

Native Seeds / SEARCH
2509 Campbell Ave. #325
Tucson, AZ 85719

The Cook's Garden
PO Box 535
Londonderry, VT 05148
802-824-3400

Seeds West
PO box 1739
El Prado, NM 87529
505-758-7268

Index

RECIPES IN ORDER OF APPEARANCE

PRODUCT INDEX

photo by Chel Beeson

Dave DeWitt is one of the foremost authorities in the world on chile peppers and spicy foods. He is the editor of *Chile Pepper Magazine,* and co-author of *The Fiery Cuisines, The Whole Chile Pepper Book* and *Callaloo, Calypso & Carnival.* Mary Jane Wilan is co-author of *The Food Lover's Handbook to the Southwest* and *Callaloo, Calypso & Carnival.* Dave and Mary Jane are the producers of the National Fiery Foods Show. They live in Albuquerque.

The Crossing Press
publishes a full
selection of cookbooks.

To receive our current catalog,
please call toll-free,
800-777-1048.